Table of Contents

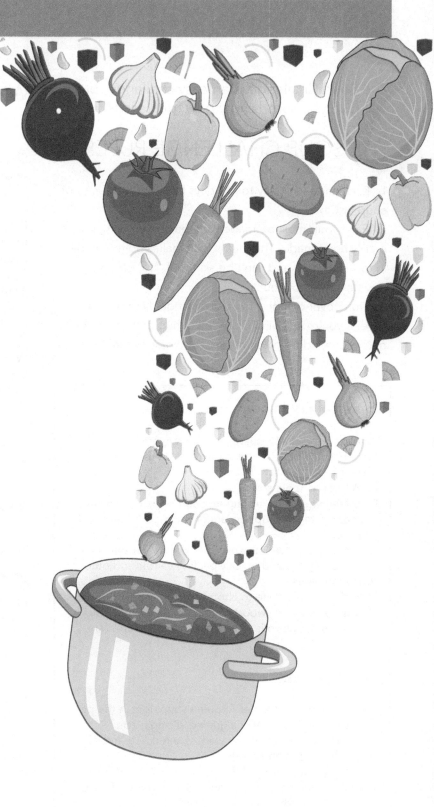

The Soup Challenge is an easy challenge, but it will give you surprisingly powerful results.

THE SOUP CHALLENGE RULES

1. **Each and every day for 30 days have at least 1 cup of soup** or broth.
2. Each soup must be made with **real meat broth**, preferably homemade. The meat broth makes up the magic in this challenge and can't be skipped! No, collagen powder does not count.
3. Don't over-complicate this challenge! Less is more here. If you're in a pinch, heat up a mug of broth in the microwave, add a pinch of salt, and enjoy before bed.

Essential Equipment:

☐ A stock pot (4-12 quart) to make stovetop broth and large batches of soup. An Instant Pot can be used in place of a stock pot.
☐ A ladle to serve soup.
☐ Something to store soup in; quart or pint mason jars are easy to re-use. Tupperware or Pyrex containers also work well.
☐ A heavy-duty vegetable peeler. A must for peeling winter squash and quickly peeling carrots and other root vegetables.
☐ A sharp chef's knife to chop veggies.
☐ One large sturdy wood cutting board. Butcher block is best, but bamboo is more economical and still very useful.

Nice to Have:

☐ An immersion blender to puree soup right in the pot.
☐ A food processor with a grating/slicing blade attachment makes quick work of shredding and slicing both veggies and cheese.
☐ A pressure canner (different than an Instant Pot) to make shelf stable broth and soup. I have a Presto Canner, All American is a great brand as well.
☐ Zip-top gallon freezer bags- They take up much less room in the freezer than jars, and won't break if dropped when slippery and frozen.
☐ A canning funnel to easily transfer batches of soup to quart or pint jars for canning or storing leftovers.

WHY DO A SOUP CHALLENGE?

Soup soup soup – delicious, flavorful, easy to digest, nourishing, frugal, quick to make, and full of amazing health benefits! Plus soup is easy!

Putting soup in the slow cooker or Instant Pot in the morning not only fills the house with a delicious aroma all day, but it also means that dinner is ready when you are and on the table in minutes. With soup made from the recipe section Soups as Meals your warm bowl of soup is a meal all on its own, or serve with a quick salad, sliced fruit, or bread.

With soup made from the recipe section Soups as Sides, you will find over a dozen soups to complement anything else on your table- from roast beef to chicken nuggets to mac n cheese!

On this 30-Day Soup Challenge, we eat soup every day and plan to continue all winter. But we start with just 30 days and go from there. You are sure to fall in love with many delicious nourishing recipes as the challenge goes on.

Weight Loss and Portion Control

While weight loss is a complicated topic, the Soup Challenge can help people who need help with portion control, and provide lots of filling vegetables, protein, and fat without empty calories or many carbohydrates.

The Soup Challenge provides much-needed nutrition in a delicious comforting soup, which calms the nervous system and allows you to absorb more needed vitamins and minerals, helping you feel more nourished and satisfied.

Having a soup starter is a great way to get the nutrition and liquid your body is craving, leaving you less hungry for junk food.

If you are eating lower carb or keto, see the keto notes for each recipe, as well as the Net Carbs in the nutrition information.

When you start the meal with a delicious nutrient-dense soup, watch and see how much easier it is to control your portions of less nutrient-dense foods.

Pictured: Autumn Vegetable Soup with Chicken, Basic Beef and Vegetable Soup, and Bacon and Black Bean Soup

FLAVORFUL SOUP
FOR AUTUMN AND WINTER

Soup combines endless flavor combinations into delicious warm meals all winter long. Page through this book if you find yourself in a meal rut, and choose something new and different to liven your meals and dark winter evenings up.

Hearty soup made with tomato such as Every Week Red Chili page 20, Basic Beef and Vegetable page 24, and Tomato Meatball Soup page 35, are comforting and hearty.

 Soup made with poultry such as Creamy Low Carb Turkey Pot Pie Soup page 48, Chicken Cordon Bleu Soup page 50, and Zesty Greek Lemon Chicken Soup page 47 are lighter in flavor, bringing pops of color to your winter table.

Legumes make delicious and economical soups on page 58, with many ways of topping and flavoring- from bacon and green onions on Black Bean Soup page 59 to a squeeze of fresh lemon in Garbanzo Lemon Soup page 60 to bright yellow turmeric and toasted coconut in Golden Lentil Soup page 57.

Sea food's delicate flavor and texture gives you much needed vitamin D in chowder, stew, and soup on page 50.

In Soups as Sides you will find new exciting flavor combinations such as butternut squash and ginger, earthy beets with spicy cayenne, mushrooms with sage, and more.

TAKE THE SOUP CHALLENGE STEP-BY-STEP

Gather Supplies & Make A Plan

Aim to have 3 quarts of broth made each week.

Learn how to make broth and, purchase either marrow bones (your health food store probably has either marrow bones, or osso buco which contains marrow) or chicken wings, drumsticks, or backs - you want to make sure it has the bones. If you don't have a good source of meat, or you just prefer the ease of having quality groceries shipped to your house, you can click here and search 'soup bones' and tons will pop up!

If you're ordering online, purchase enough meat for the month:

I recommend the following for variety and nourishment, you can find these cuts at US Wellness Meats online, at healthhomeandhappiness.com/uswellness

Use 1-2 pounds of soup bones/meat per 1 gallon of water or one large broth/instant pot.

So one week you'd use chicken backs, the second week you'd do marrow bones, the third you'd do a beef knuckle, etc.

- 2 pounds chicken backs or necks
- 2 pounds beef marrow bones, any kind (I usually choose whatever is cheapest)
- 1 beef knuckle (really!)
- 2 pounds alternative broth bones/meat (bison marrow bones, lamb osso bucco, etc)
- Optional but helpful, one of their 2.5 lb pails of chicken broth to have in your freezer in case you run out.

Organize your week:

Once a week, write out you meal plan using your own or filling in a copy of the meal plan in this book. Download extra copies to print at https://soupchallenge.net

The meal plan can be as simple or as complicated as you like. At a minimum, include 2 soups that you will make for the week. Add any ingredients needed to your weekly grocery list, grocery shop, and make a fresh batch of broth.

Prepare for the unexpected

Buy Shelf Stable Broth:
If you have less time but are willing to spend some money to make this happen (you'll probably recover it in less sick days), Kettle and Fire has healing broth that I absolutely approve of. The regular broth on the grocery store shelves is more like chicken-flavored water and doesn't have the healing benefits of traditionally made broth. Purchasing some from Kettle and Fire can be great for traveling (it is shelf stable) or as a backup as well.
Find their soup at healthhomeandhappiness.com/broth

Buy pre-made healing soups:
If you really need a shortcut, Kettle and Fire also has pre-made nourishing soup! All you need to do then is heat up a package every day, and you'll get all the benefits of the challenge, with a heat-and-serve convenience!

Note to those on the GAPS Diet: Kettle and Fire soup has trace starches in it, and is not GAPS legal. Their broth is great for GAPS though! If you're not on GAPS, Kettle and Fire soup is GREAT. It's just that GAPS people need to avoid any trace of starches.

Prep Notes:
- Make sure you have real broth on hand, more than you think you need! Make more each week.
- Even if you intend to use fresh veggies, grab a few bags of frozen broccoli, cauliflower, butternut squash, and/or mixed veggies just in case.

Make & Enjoy Your Soups for 30 days

I know how much we can need and want to change our eating habits, but all the programs and overhauls can feel SO overwhelming! That's why we're doing this challenge... This isn't a 'live only on soup' challenge, it's simply adding one serving (1 cup for adults, it can be less for kids) of nourishing soup to what you normally eat every day.

The truth is that even though we live with access to amazing foods in the US, a lot of us are nutrient starved! That's where this soup comes in, it contains a concentrated dose of all those missing nutrients from the Standard American Diet. (yes, I do know that some of you on this challenge aren't from the US, but most are).

By challenging yourself to consume a burst of nutrition every single day, you'll remind your body how good it feels to be nourished. This sets you up for long-term success.

See the Results!

The 30-Day Soup Challenge not only gives us results nutritionally, but it also establishes a comforting rhythm in the kitchen that promotes connection with each other and our food, as well as a routine to make delicious food preparation automatic all winter long.

My readers have reported the following results through the soup challenge:

• Better sleep, even for previously restless sleepers

• Smooth skin- This is the #1 email I get from you! It's the broth, baby... broth is so good for skin!

• Kids that are calmer during meal time since they're starting their meals with a warm nourishing food

• Kids that branch out and try foods you never thought they would!

• Grocery savings! – Some of you report over $100 in grocery savings just by adding soup to each meal!

Date:		Directions: Keep yourself on track by numbering the days you've had soup! *Optional*: Record and Rate the soup you enjoyed that day.

	Week 1	Week 2	Week 3	Week 4	Week 5
Mon	*Example:* *Day 1 Carrot and* *Cauliflower Soup* *****				
Tue					
Wed					
Thu					
Fri					
Sat					
Sun					

Notes: This optional weekly meal schedule can help you plan out your meals, groceries and the soups you want to try.

Week:

Monday

Breakfast	
Lunch	
Dinner	
Snack	

Tuesday

Breakfast	
Lunch	
Dinner	
Snack	

Wednesday

Breakfast	
Lunch	
Dinner	
Snack	

Thursday

Breakfast	
Lunch	
Dinner	
Snack	

Friday

Breakfast	
Lunch	
Dinner	
Snack	

Saturday

Breakfast	
Lunch	
Dinner	
Snack	

Sunday

Breakfast	
Lunch	
Dinner	
Snack	

Groceries

STORING AND REHEATING SOUP

Soup stores really well and reheats well whether on the stove or in the microwave. A thermos food jar makes lunches a snap to pack, and keep your soup cozy warm until lunch or dinner when you're away from home.

You may be surprised that I use the microwave to re-heat soup often. If I'm serving the whole family leftover soup, I usually reheat the soup on the stovetop, but for just myself or just one serving, I pour into a mug or bowl and microwave on high for a minute and all is well!

Shop:

Optional items that can make your Soup Challenge easier. Remember, leftovers are lovely with the Soup Challenge!

- Thermos, Food Jar Style
- Canning (Mason) Jars
- Canning funnel for easy transfer from a stock pot to mason jar.

PACKING THERMOSES

To keep soup hot and ready for a meal away from home, there are 3 steps:

1. Pre-heat your thermos. Run your sink until your tap water is very hot, and put hot water in your thermos. I do this as I'm heating the soup (on the stove or in the microwave) and then dump the water right before filling with soup.

2. As your thermos is pre-heating with hot water, heat your soup in the microwave or on the stovetop. If your soup has any dairy in it (cream, cheese) make sure it does not boil or the texture will become clumpy.

3. Fill your thermos at least 3/4 full with your hot soup. Top with the lid and enjoy your soup-on-the-go!

SOUP LEFTOVERS

Strategic leftovers are key to what makes the Soup Challenge so effective! Soup leftovers are even better the next day as the flavors have had time to meld.

Soups are easy lunches, and can be stored in mason jars or single-portion glass containers for easy single-serving reheating.

Keys to Good Soup Leftovers:

- If your soup has dairy (cream, cheese, milk) make sure it is gently re-heated and does NOT come to a boil after the dairy has been added. If it comes to a boil it's not dangerous to eat, but the texture will be grainy.

- If you have extra chili, but not enough for another full meal, it is a great addition to hotdogs (we like Teton Waters' grassfed or Applegate organic) for chili dogs! Chili is also delicious on baked potatoes, nachos, and over corn bread.

- Avoid over-heating soup with green vegetables in it, particularly broccoli-cheddar, to keep it from turning mushy.

Freezer Meals

If you like to really get ahead of the game, you can prep a bunch of soups for the freezer at once. We have a special Instant Soup Packs section on page 85 for detailed instructions.

A few things to keep in mind as you freezer prep:

- Blanch, bake, or steam veggies before freezing so they keep their flavor. This doesn't have to be long, they just need to get above 120* F. A good rule is that if veggies are too hot to touch, they are hot enough to have killed the enzymes. Enzymes are what causes vegetables to break down in the freezer.

- Making broth cubes (page 17) is a great time and space saver! These cubes can be added to pre-cut vegetables, or even bags of frozen veggies for instant soups!

- If prepping meat, browning the meat before freezing or canning is an important step.

  Browning a bunch of meat at once saves not only your time, but also leaves you cleaning up grease splatters only once! Putting un-browned meat into soup can be done, but the texture and flavor won't be nearly as good.

GETTING CHILDREN TO ENJOY SOUP

It's good for children to see us cook, and the lesson of working now so that you can reap the benefits later will carry them through to adulthood.

Different children and different families have different needs. So do whatever works for your family. Here are some suggestions for involving the kids during your 30-Day Soup Challenge.

Establishing Habits

When kids help with dinner, they are learning that cooking from scratch is normal and they are tucking kitchen skills such as browning meat and chopping onions into the automatic part of their brain.

This sets them up for success later in life, when it's just automatic to thaw the meat you need for dinner in the morning and stand over the stove browning meat for dinner. Most kids like soup, it has so many flavors, the texture can be smooth if preferred, and there are toppings! Having some soup every day all winter helps with dry skin and mucus membranes, healthy sleep, and a healthy immune system.

The nourishing broth in soup also provides easy nutrition to heal the gut lining and actually will help rebalance the gut flora to help your child select healthy foods instead of junk food!

Your grandmother was right, give your child broth to boost their health and vitality!

ROUTINES

The process of making soup is very routine-based, which even young babies and toddlers enjoy. The routine of making soup with the cold months carries into childhood (and adulthood!) and is a familiar pattern in the kitchen.

The routine of regular soup-making comes from making the broth in preparation of making soup, and even before that saving the bones and carcasses from meat, along with veggie scraps. This step is both the foundational step for your soup and the foundational step for your kitchen in using all parts of your food.

Next, when making soup we start nearly every soup the same way- melt some fat, add in onions and/or garlic, and sautee. Cut up the meat, chop the veggies. Stir and cover in broth and simmer.

Last, we serve soup often as an appetizer- making sure hungry bellies are first filled with the most nutritious food. You will see children mimic this entire process in their play kitchen, or on the floor using empty pots and pans from the cupboard.

TOPPINGS

Turning through these pages, you see how many hearty, fun, and whimsical toppings you can add to each soup! Kiddos love this, and since our toppings are also nutrient-dense, you can happily allow them to top their soup as desired. This gives the kiddos a feeling of autonomy, control, and even creative expression with their food.

Ranch dressing (page 28) is a favorite topper in our house, along with 'bacon sprinkles' (crumbled bacon). Snipping fresh chives is fun for young scissor-users, and shredding cheese is a great job to keep older children involved in the cooking process.

FIRST THIS THEN THAT

Getting children to want to eat nutritious food when they are surrounded by junk food in commercials and at the school lunch table can be a balancing act.

Rather than have the dinner table be a battle ground (which is not good for anyone's digestion!), I find saying 'yes, when' works better for us. Yes, you can have ice cream after you've eaten this (small) portion of dinner. Yes, you can have more rice, but please eat another serving of soup first. Yes, we can make cookies this weekend and you can have a couple after dinner then.

When we structure the meal so the most nourishing food is served first, our kids fill up on the good stuff. I have my kids eat soup prior to eating other dishes such as rice, bread, or even fruit. Then I know they have a good amount of protein, produce, and fat in their system.

As we all know, eating nourishing food really does feel better in our bellies, and usually once you get a child to start, and break down their defenses by saying that 'yes' they also can have their desired food, they eat more of the good stuff than usual.

More tips that work for us:

- Start with small portions- a custard cup of soup rather than a whole bowl. This gets kids in the habit of actually requesting more of what is good for them.
- Don't focus on the negative! We banish negative talk and complaints from the dinner table, and keep that time positive for good digestion. A favorite game we play while we eat is to go around the table and talk

SPECIAL DIETARY NEEDS

Dietary needs are so individual that I would never be able to create a one-size-fits-all solution, but the good news is that most of the soups in this book are allergen friendly! Here we look at common swaps and considerations as we go through the Soup Challenge Cookbook.

GLUTEN-FREE

Good news! Every soup in this book is gluten free!

PALEO DIET

Most recipes in this book are appropriate for a paleo diet. Omit beans, and use the dairy-free adaptations if applicable.

KETO and LOW CARB

Many of the soups in this book are acceptable on the keto and low carb diets. Net carbs are included in the nutrition facts (total carbohydrate minus indigestible fiber)

Suggestions: Cut in half the amount of tomatoes, onions, and carrots in the recipes to further lower the carb counts.

GAPS DIET

Most of the soups in this book are GAPS friendly. If there are needed changes, see the notes on each recipe.

Common changes: Use white beans in place of any other bean called for.
Use yogurt cheese in place of cream cheese.
Make your ranch dressing homemade.

NIGHTSHADE-FREE

Tomato-based soups aren't appropriate for those avoiding nightshades. Replace tomato paste with pumpkin puree, and omit diced tomatoes and peppers from recipes.

DAIRY-FREE

Many recipes in this book are dairy-free or dairy-optional. If dairy is just a garnish or topping, omit cheese and use coconut milk or coconut cream in place of cream or sour cream.

VEGETARIAN/VEGAN

Unfortunately, the Soup Challenge and Soup Challenge cookbook are not appropriate for the vegetarian or vegan. The base of the soups in this book is always meat stock made with real meat.

BROTH BASICS

BROTH VS STOCK

If you look on my website, you see that I refer to broth and stock interchangeably throughout Health Home and Happiness. For clarity in this book, we always use *broth* in our recipes.

Broth is gentle on the digestive system and contains many easily-absorbed amino acids to build and repair cells. Broth can be made, as described in these following pages, or it is also produced by baking meat- the drippings that accumulate in the baking dish also qualify as broth (save these and add them to your broth jars or soups!)

Broth is made from meat and can have bones in the meat.

Stock is made with just bones.

I do make stock too, especially when a lot of the connective tissue is still present. Stock has a long simmer time usually, to extract the last bits of flavor and nutrition from bones before discarding.

SPECIAL EQUIPMENT:

All you really need is a large pot that can hold at least 3 quarts of water, a way to strain your broth (a colander), and something to store your broth in.

Many of us also enjoy using our pressure cooker and/or slow cooker, so the following pages will detail different broth-making methods using these appliances as well.

Broth-Making Methods

Instant Pot broth is the most clear, presumably because the pressure involved keeps the hot broth from vigorously boiling.

The stock pot broth is most cloudy, as above, because the simmering broke apart small parts of the meat and vegetables, and some air has been incorporated as well.

The slow cooker broth, despite its longer cook time, produced broth that was lighter than Instant Pot. This could be due to including less onion peels, or because we didn't brown the meat before covering with water. All beef broths were equally delicious, had equal fat content at the top after chilling, and had equal gelling properties.

All the beef meat/cartilage/bones were saved for reuse and there did not appear to be any noticeable difference in the quality of them between the appliances.

Tip: As you go through the Soup Challenge, keep a gallon freezer zip-top bag in the freezer with anything you want to add to your next batch of broth:

- Carrot Tops, broccoli stems, and any other clean veggie trimming.
- Onion Skins (clean)
- Bones and trimmings from meat (like the carcass from a rotisserie chicken, lamb bones from lamb chops, the gristle you cut off from a steak)

Beef Broth

Grassfed organic beef broth, rich in amino acids from the beef bones, collagen, and meat; rich in vitamins and minerals from the produce scraps and sea salt; and rich in phytonutrients from ginger and garlic! This amazing gut-healing health-giving food is nearly free to make, and takes very little time.

Ingredients:

1-2 pounds Grassfed Beef Soup Bones: *Oxtail, osso buco, marrow bones, knuckle, shank bones- something that has both bone and meat and lots of that cartilage that will be turned into rich nourishing broth*

Filtered Water (tap water or bottled water is just fine if you don't have a filter)

Sea Salt

Clean Vegetable Scraps, particularly onion peels to make broth a beautiful golden color (optional)

2-3 cloves garlic (optional)

1-2 inches ginger root (optional)

Stove top (classic recipe):

1. Heat your stock pot on a large burner over medium-high heat. Allow pot to preheat for a minute or two, and then add your soup bones (keep the meat on if they came with meat). Do not use the lid for this step. Allow meat/bones to brown for 10-15 minutes and then turn.
2. Add optional vegetable scraps, garlic, ginger, and then fill broth pot 3/4 full with filtered water. Do not add the salt yet.
3. Bring to a boil over medium-high heat, and then reduce to a simmer (this is about a '2' on my stove, you'll get to know what is a simmer on your stove, they all vary a bit). Once broth is on a low simmer, cover to keep heat in and reduce cooking time by a little bit.
4. Simmer for 3-12 hours, as desired. Broth is done when it is a rich golden color, and all vegetable scraps are well cooked, and cartilage on the marrow bone is starting to soften. Cooking the broth longer will extract more beneficial amino acids from the cartilage surrounding the bones.
5. Remove lid and allow broth to cool a bit, so it is not so dangerous to pour.

Slow Cooker:

1. Place soup bones in slow cooker. Add optional vegetable scraps, garlic, ginger, and then fill the ceramic crock 3/4 full with filtered water. Do not add the salt yet.
2. Turn slow cooker to low and allow to cook 8-24 hours, as desired. Broth is done when it is a rich golden color, and all vegetable scraps are well cooked, and cartilage on the marrow bone is starting to soften. Cooking the broth longer will extract more beneficial amino acids from the cartilage surrounding the bones.
3. Turn slow cooker off and allow broth to cool a bit, so it is not so dangerous to pour.

Instant Pot:

1. Turn your Instant Pot to Saute - and Adjust to Medium heat. Allow pot to preheat for a minute or two, and then add your soup bones (keep the meat on if they came with meat). Do not use the lid for this step. Allow meat/bones to brown for 10-15 minutes and then turn. Turn Instant Pot off after turning, but keep the meat in there.
2. Add optional vegetable scraps, garlic, ginger, and then fill to the 'max' line on the stainless steel pot with filtered water. Do not add the salt yet.
3. Place lid on and adjust valve to 'seal'. Set Instant Pot to Manual, 90 minutes. Instant pot will come to pressure and then turn off on its own. After cooking, allow pressure to release naturally, this can take up to 30 minutes.
4. Remove lid and allow broth to cool a bit, so it is not so dangerous to pour.

Continue for all methods:

1. Remove meat, bones, and cartilage (save for another batch). Poke marrow out of the middle of the bone and add to your finished broth. Discard vegetable scraps.
2. Pour broth into jars using a funnel, or simmer down to reduce the broth as desired. (see more details of this reduction process here.
3. Add salt as desired, I use a scant 1 teaspoon per quart of unreduced broth, which helps preserve the broth but will not become overpowering if the broth is reduced, like in a sauce.
4. Store broth in the refrigerator for up to 3 weeks, or in the freezer for 1 year, or pressure can (page 17).

CHICKEN BROTH

Chicken broth is a traditionally healing food and thought by some to be easier to digest than beef broth.

The flavor of chicken broth is lighter than beef broth, though I happily use the broth flavors interchangeably in recipes.

Don't feel nervous if you have to substitute chicken broth for beef broth in any of the recipes in this book- they will still taste delicious.

2 lbs Chicken with bones and skin: Wings, bone-in thighs, drumsticks, the carcass of a whole chicken, or even necks, or backs
  Optional: 4 cloves garlic, 2-4 cups of veggie scraps, 2 inches fresh ginger root

Stovetop (Stockpot) Directions

1. Bake chicken in stainless steel stock pot at 400° for 30 minutes, or until juices on the bottom start to brown. This will deepen the flavor and color in the finished broth.
2. Move pot with browned chicken to the stovetop.

Instant Pot Directions

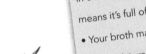

1. Brown in the Instant Pot using the Saute function *(medium setting)* for 5 minutes on each side.
2. After the chicken is browned, add optional garlic, veggie scraps, and ginger root. Fill broth pot or Instant Pot 3/4 full of water to cover the chicken and veggie scraps. Cook on manual for 90 minutes. Allow pressure to release naturally.

Continue for either method:

1. After the broth has been removed from heat, *(optional)* allow to cool until it isn't super hot (about an hour). Place a colander in a large bowl, and pour the broth out, catching the chicken pieces and veggie scraps in the colander. Do in multiple batches if needed. If not making optional broth cubes, transfer broth to large jars and store in the fridge for up to 2 weeks.

Broth Colors and Textures

• Your broth will gel (turn solid or thicken) in the fridge, this is normal and GOOD! It means it's full of protein.

• Your broth may be more or less pale than what is pictured here. That is usually based on the amount of **onion skins** in the broth. No matter the color, it's good for you and delicious in all the recipes in this book!

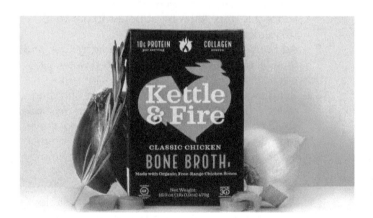

Buying Broth

When we make broth, we're using real meat, and hopefully marrow too. Don't confuse homemade broth with the meat-flavored water that you can buy in cartons at the store. Homemade broth is rich in protein and fat, the store-bought (or worse yet, bouillon cubes!) is flavored of meat, but void of most of the nutrition.

If you want to have some store-bought on hand for traveling or when you're in a pinch, I recommend Kettle & Fire. It's homemade broth, in a carton.

BROTH CUBES

Tip: The extra step of making broth cubes keeps your fridge and freezer from being overwhelmed with broth, and makes broth instantly available to add to rice, stir fry, or just heat up for a warm mug of delicious nutrition on a cold day!

2 quarts broth (or more)
1/4 cup beef gelatin

1. Return to the desired amount of stock pot or Instant Pot and simmer down for another hour, until reduced to 2 cups (reduced by 3/4). For the Instant Pot you will do this using the Saute function with the lid off.

2. Once broth has been reduced, allow to cool to room temperature again. Once at room temperature add 1/4 cup beef gelatin and stir in. Allow the gelatin to absorb the liquid for 5 minutes, stir with a whisk to break up any clumps, and then heat over medium heat for 10 minutes or until the gelatin is transparent and melted.

3. Again cool to room temp, then pour into a casserole dish or just put the entire pot in the fridge over night.

4. Once firm, run a butter knife around the outside of the block of broth/gelatin and pop out the entire block onto a cutting board. Use a large chef's knife to cut into 2-inch cubes, or desired size.

5. Place cubes in a gallon zip-top bag in a single layer and lay flat to freeze. If you think of it *(set a reminder on your phone!)* before you go to bed flip the bag over and wiggle the cubes so they don't freeze together in one big block. If you forget this step you can still pop them off each other pretty easily.

6. To use, add water to one cube to make one cup. This replaces 1 cup of broth in recipes.

PRESSURE CANNING BROTH

Tip: Pressure canning makes broth shelf stable and easy to store and transport, as long as you have room for glass jars. It's really that easy to use- just open a jar and heat and drink or add to a recipe! Learn more about pressure canning at the end of this book.

2 quarts broth (or more), adjust the amount of jars you use to accommodate
2 teaspoons sea salt

1. Pre-heat jars and lids to hot but not boiling.
2. Pre-heat pressure canner over medium heat with 3-4 quarts water, or the amount indicated by your pressure canner's manual.
3. Add hot broth to each jar, leaving 1 inch at the top. This is called head space.
4. Add 1/2 teaspoon sea salt (optional) to each pint jar.
5. Use a towel dipped in vinegar to wipe the rim of each filled jar. Top with lids and screw on bands until firmly secured but not over tightened. As tight as you can get them without really forcing anything is just fine.
6. Place hot jars in hot canner and secure lid on canner. Turn heat to medium-high.
7. Once steam is coming out of the vent pipe, allow to vent with steam coming out for 10 minutes.
8. Cover the vent pipe with the counter weight (dial gauges) or weighted gauge (jiggler)
9. Once proper pressure is reached, process for indicated time below.
10. After the time has been reached at the proper pressure, remove from heat by either lifting off the electric burner or turning off the gas.
11. Allow canner to de-pressurize on its own, do not open the vent pipe. This takes about 30-45 minutes.
12. Once depressurized, remove jars carefully and allow to cool 1 inch apart on a cooling rack or folded towel. Once cool check lids for seal. If they are sealed, your broth is now good for 1 year at room temperature! Remove rings before storing.

Pressure:
Under 1,000 feet 10 lbs
Over 1,000 feet 15 lbs

Time:
Pint jars 20 minutes,
Quart jars: 25 minutes

If mixing pint and quart jars, process all jars for the longer time

THE 'DRINK YOUR BROTH' SICK-NESS POLICY

Are they really sick, or are they trying to get out of chores/school/eating Sunday's vegetables? This question pops up often during cold and flu season, even more when we have more than one child. How do you both honor when your child is actually sick, and avoid giving in to little white lies?

Enter the Broth Sickness Policy!

What is the Broth Sick Policy?

The broth sick policy is our household sickness policy. In our home if you are too sick to do your responsibilities, we want to ensure that you are getting the nutrition, fluids, and electrolytes your body needs to heal itself.

The rule is simple: If you opt out of doing something because you are sick, you must drink a mug of broth before you have your meal.

The broth sick policy continues for 1 meal after we've returned to being able to do our responsibilities, because good nutrition is important for newly-recovered bodies as well.

This is especially true if you are missing school because you are sick. I'm happy to keep you home so you can rest and recover, but because you're feeling so run down, we need to provide a good source of nutrition.

Because I'm the mom, and I'm in charge, I decide how big the mug is based on how much I think the child is faking. A truely sick child often gets our little bird mug half filled before they have a few bites of dinner. A child I suspect is looking to opt out of a math test or seeing if they can watch TV all day rather than fold their laundry gets a bigger mug.

As with all my mealtime parenting, we don't negotiate-whether it's the size of the mug or anything else. The children know what's expected of them up front, and our broth really is delicious anyway, so I feel no guilt requiring this of them.

Why broth?

Broth is the number one super food in our home! When you boil meat and connective tissue and especially bone marrow into water, the amino acids from the meat become broken down and dissolved into the water for super easy digestion by the gut!

Add in a squeeze of lemon for both flavor and vitamin C, and a pinch of salt again for flavor and electrolytes, and you've got yourself the best sickness remedy ever!

What if my child won't eat at all?

This depends if it is a medical issue or not. Of course I'm not advocating starving out your children or allow them to become dehydrated. But I do question the validity of getting kids to eat 'anything' when they are sick rather than very little.

That said, I allow my children to skip meals and rest while they are sick. And once they are up to eating again, they get broth before every meal until they feel better.

Yes, they do lose weight. In my experience, all children that are ill lose weight – and giving a few calories of popsicle or sugary treat really doesn't change that but may very well prolong how long they are sick.

When I'm sick my appetite is much lower as well. This lowered appetite allows the body to have more energy for fighting off the illness, and always returns for my children following an illness.

Often parents are so afraid of their children not eating for the time they are sick that they push sugary popsicles, soda, and crackers on them – anything that they'll eat. I've never done this, and I'm perfectly comfortable allowing my children's naturally lowered appetite during true sickness to run its course.

Of course this is dependant on your child and your family situation, and won't work for everyone.

SOUPS AS MEALS: RECIPES

EVERY-WEEK RED CHILI

MAKES 8 SERVINGS

As soon as the weather cools down in the fall we have this chili weekly for at least a couple months! It's one of the first recipes my kids learn to make independently, they love it!

Adding liver in ensures we are getting needed iron, vitamins A and D, and all the Bs needed for health and growth. The chili flavor covers the liver well, but if you're concerned, use more mild chicken liver instead of beef liver or omit liver completely.

This recipe makes a lot of chili, perfect for feeding a crowd, or for leftovers. Leftovers are delicious re-heated, added to grassfed hotdogs for chili dogs, or on top of tortilla chips or pork skins for nachos.

1/4 cup butter or olive oil
3 cloves garlic, crushed
1 onion, chopped
3 pounds ground beef
1/2 pound beef or chicken liver
1 tablespoon ground cumin
3 tablespoons chili powder
1 pinch cinnamon
1 cup kidney beans, soaked overnight, see below
2 1/2 cups+ beef broth
8 ounces canned tomato paste OR 16 ounces diced tomatoes
1 tablespoon sea salt
1 tablespoon honey

To serve:
1 cup finely chopped fresh cilantro (optional)
Grated cheddar cheese
Sour Cream
Additional chopped onion, sliced jalapenos, and chopped cilantro to garnish

PREPARE LIVER

1. Drain any blood from thawed liver. Place in a bowl. Cover with the juice of one lemon and filtered water until the liver is completely covered. Cover bowl with lid or plastic wrap and return to the fridge. Soaking the liver removes the blood and bitterness.
2. To cook, pan fry in 1 teaspoon fat (coconut oil, butter, ghee, etc) over medium heat, 5 minutes on each side. Allow to cool and crumble or chop into 1/4 inch cubes for recipe.

Note: Chicken liver is most mildly flavored, but beef and lamb liver are hidden surprisingly well in chili.

SOAK BEANS

1. Rinse kidney beans in a colander, removing any rocks or debris that may be in the package.
2. Place beans in a large bowl (they will swell to triple their current size) and cover with filtered water so that they are covered by an inch or more. Allow to soak for 24 hours, changing the water once during this timeperiod.
3. This reduces the starch content of the beans and makes them easier to digest.

FOR THE CHILI

1. Melt butter in a large Dutch oven, stock pot, or Instant Pot over medium heat. Add crushed garlic and chopped onion and saute for 10 minutes, until aromatic.
2. Add in ground beef and liver and brown until beef is cooked through, stirring often and breaking up beef with back of spoon, about 10 minutes.
3. If using a slow cooker, transfer to the slow cooker now and continue with the rest of the recipe in the slow cooker.
4. Add cumin, chili powder, and soaked beans to the cooked meat.
5. Mix in 2 1/2 cups chicken broth, tomato paste, honey, and 1/2 cup cilantro.

6. Cook (choose of the following 3 methods)

   Stovetop: Reduce heat to medium-low and cover with a lid, cook 1 1/2 hours on stovetop, adding more water by 1/4 cupfuls if chili becomes dry.

    Slow cooker: Cover and cook on low for 6-8 hours.

   Instant Pot: Place the lid on the Instant Pot, set to seal, and cook under pressure (manual) for 45 minutes. Allow pressure to release naturally before lifting lid.
7. Season with salt and pepper.
8. Mix remaining 1/2 cup cilantro into chili.
9. Ladle chili into bowls.
10. Serve, topping with cheese, sour cream and additional chopped onion and sliced jalapenos as desired.

Recipe makes 8 Servings
Calories 654 Fat 42g Carbohydrates 26g Fiber 6g Protein 43g
Vitamin A 6435IU (129% DV) Iron 8mg (44% DV)

Recipe made without beans for keto and paleo, still 8 servings:
Calories 577 Fat 42g Carbohydrates 12g Fiber 3g Sugar 6g Protein 38g
Vitamin A 6435IU (129% DV) Iron 7mg (39% DV) *9 g net Carbs

SPECIAL DIET NOTES:
For GAPS use navy beans (white beans) and soak for the full 24-hours as instructed.

Paleo and Keto: Omit beans completely.

PEPPERONI PIZZA CHILI

Another variation of chili, this time without the beans, but with favorite pizza flavors. Toppings make for a fun custom dinner, set out any favorite pizza toppings (yes, even pineapple tidbits if desired for your kiddo!) and this chili packs in a lot of protein and a lot of fun!

Makes: 4 Servings Prep time: 15 minutes Cook time: 30 minutes

1 pound beef or pork sausage
6 oz mushrooms
1 large onion
1 large bell pepper
2 cups chicken or beef broth
12 ounces tomato paste (2 small cans)
1 teaspoon sea salt+ more to taste
1 tablespoon fresh parsley
1 teaspoon fresh thyme
1/2 teaspoon dried oregano
1/4 teaspoon cayenne

Optional:
4 oz black olives
1/2 cup mozzarella cheese
1 ounce pepperoni

INSTRUCTIONS

1. In the bottom of a large sauce pan or small stock pot over medium heat, brown sausage until nearly cooked through.
2. Rinse and slice mushrooms.
3. Rinse and chop pepper and onion.
4. Add mushrooms, bell pepper, and onion to the sausage and continue to brown until soft.
5. Keep over medium heat and add in the broth, tomato paste, sea salt, and herbs and stir to combine.
6. Reduce heat to a simmer, and simmer for 20 minutes, or until hot and bubbly, stirring every few minutes.
7. To get pepperoni that is crispy, like what's on the top of pizza, fry thinly sliced pepperoni for a couple minutes over medium heat in a single layer in a skillet. Flip to brown both sides, then set aside and top chili with the crisp pepperoni.
8. Spoon into bowls and top with cheese and additional fresh herbs and chopped olives if desired.
9. Enjoy!

Nutrition per serving (4 servings per recipe) Calories 569 Fat 42g Carbohydrates 24g Fiber 6g Protein 28g

Net carbs= 18 g

Serving Tip: A pizza chili bar is fun for feeding a crowd. Set out small bowls with conventional pizza toppings (pepperoni, cheese, anchovies, pineapple, olives, etc) and then let people add their favorites to their chili!

GAPS Notes: watch ingredients in the pepperoni and sausage. It's possible to find GAPS-legal sausage and pepperoni in most grocery stores. If needed, use unseasoned ground pork or beef instead of the sausage.

BASIC GROUND BEEF AND VEGETABLE SOUP

This basic soup is delicious, filling, inexpensive, and made with easy-to-find ingredients. The extra portion of ground beef makes it extra filling! Don't let the 'basic' in the title fool you- we make this all the time and we all love it!

Makes 6 Servings

2 tablespoons butter or avocado oil
1 yellow onion peeled and chopped
2 pounds ground beef
2 teaspoons sea salt
1/2 teaspoon ground black pepper
1/2 teaspoon dried thyme optional
1/4 teaspoon dried oregano optional
2 carrots
4 stalks celery
4-6 cups beef broth
14 ounces canned diced tomatoes not drained, or one pound fresh tomatoes, chopped and seeds removed

1. In a stock pot or Instant Pot using the saute function, heat butter or avocado oil over medium heat. Add chopped onion.

2. Cook onion until transluscent, stirring every few minutes to keep from sticking, about 10 minutes.

3. Leave onions in the pot, and add in ground beef, sea salt, ground blaack pepper, optional thyme and oregano.

4. Brown ground beef and break up into small chunks.

5. As the beef browns, chop carrots and celery into 1/4-inch slices, discarding ends.

6. Continue cooking ground beef until the outside of the beef starts to brown, but there is no need to cook through as it will continue cooking with the soup.

7. Add the sliced celery, carrots, beef broth, and diced tomatoes.

8. Bring to a simmer over medium-high heat, and then reduce heat, cover, and continue simmering at medium-low for 20 minutes, or until carrots are soft and beef is cooked through.

9. Top with grated parmesan cheese or enjoy as is.

Nutrition (1/6 recipe): Calories 690 Fat 52g Carbohydrates 11g Fiber 3g Net Carbs: 8g Protein 43g

Net Carbs: 9 g

SHORTCUTS FOR NOW AND LATER:

This recipe is even faster if you have pre-cooked ground beef, either frozen or canned. Use baby carrots and canned tomatoes for further shortcuts.

This recipe is great fresh, and leftovers are really good here too. Making a double batch and keeping some of this soup in the freezer makes a busy winter day so much better. Basic Ground Beef and Vegetable Soup can be canned and it's one of my favorites for the pantry! See page 82 for instructions.

HEALTH HOME & HAPPINESS

BACON CHEESEBURGER IN PARADISE SOUP

Prep time: 30 minutes Cook Time: 30 minutes Servings: 6

Mmmm, cheeseburgers! In my opinion, grilled onions are the best part of this soup, though my children greatly appreciate it when that is the optional part. I don't mind, it's more for me! Sliced avocado or guaca-mole, cheese, and bacon bits make this a cheeseburger classic.

4 slices bacon
1 pound ground beef
2 onions cut into slices/rings
2 carrots shredded
2 ribs celery sliced thinly
2 cloves garlic
1 teaspoon dried basil
1 teaspoon dried parsley flakes
3 cups beef broth
5 ounce can tomato paste or 1 medium can diced tomatoes
1 teaspoon salt
1/2 teaspoon pepper
1 cup shredded cheddar cheese
1 avocado thinly sliced

INSTRUCTIONS

1. Cook bacon in a large saucepan over medium heat.

2. Remove bacon once cooked through and leave grease in the pan.

3. Add onion rings and cook over medium-low for about 20 minutes, or until caramelized. This step does take a while, you may want to start the beef in another pan. If you're not in a hurry, remove the caramelized onions once done and set aside.

4. In the same pan, cook and crumble beef.

5. Once beef starts to brown, add in carrots, celery, garlic, basil and parsley until vegetables are tender and beef is browned, about 10 minutes.

6. Add broth, tomato paste, and salt, bring to a boil. Reduce heat; simmer, covered, 10-12 minutes.

7. After simmering, adjust salt and add pepper to taste.

8. Ladle soup into bowls, topping with the shredded cheddar cheese, caramelized onions, crumbled bacon, and avocado slices.

9. Serve with a side of pickles.

Dairy-Free Option: Omit cheese

Nutrition: Calories 435 Fat 32g Carbohydrates 14g Fiber 4g Protein 22g

Net carbs: 10 g per serving

DAIRY-FREE RANCH DRESSING

This easy ranch dressing tastes better than store-bought! It passes the taste test for even picky kids.

1 cup avocado-oil mayonnaise
1 tablespoon dried chives
1 teaspoon dried parsley
2 cloves garlic, crushed
¼ of a white onion, minced
Pinch of white pepper
¼ teaspoon salt
Coconut milk as needed to thin

1. Blend seasonings into 1 cup mayonnaise. Add 1-4 tablespoons coconut milk to reach desired consistency.
2. Cover and refrigerate at least an hour before serving, use within 7 days.

HOMEMADE TACO SEASONING

Fillers in commercial taco seasoning include things like wheat flour, milk solids (both problematic for allergies!), maltodextrin, corn starch, soybean oil, silica dioxide, and more. Your food will taste better with this easy homemade mix, and you'll feel better too!

2 tablespoons chili powder
1 tablespoon cumin
2 teaspoons salt
¼ teaspoon black pepper
1/8 teaspoon cayenne pepper

Combine all spices in a small glass jar. Store in a cupboard and use as needed.

CULTURED DILL PICKLES

Making cultured pickles is an easy delicious way to get dairy-free probiotics for easy digestion.

2 pounds small cucumbers
1-1/2 teaspoons sea salt
1 tablespoon fresh dill or 1 teaspoon dried
2 tablespoons liquid from a previously successful ferment, such as Bubbies brand pickles
Filtered water

1. Rinse cucumbers. Place in a quart jar..
2. Add sea salt, dill, and liquid from previous ferment.
3. Fill jar to within 1/2 inch of top of the jar with filtered water. Cover with air tight lid.
4. Allow to culture on countertop in a cool-but-not-cold place for 5 days, transfer to fridge once pickles start to darken in color. They are ready to eat now!

CREAMY LOW-CARB TACO SOUP

Prep time: 20 minutes. Cook Time: 1 hour Servings: 10

This low-carb Mexican-flavored taco soup brings all the flavor of tacos to your soup bowl! Make extra, you're going to love this for the next day or two leftover as well. Like our dairy-free version of Taco Soup, this soup is flavorful, but this one is also creamy and rich with the addition of cheddar and cream cheese.

Dairy-fee? See a similar delicious soup on the next page.

1 tablespoon butter or avocado oil, ghee, or other fat
1 onion
2 pounds ground beef
3 tablespoons taco seasoning
2 14-ounce cans diced tomatoes
4 cups beef broth
3/4 cup ranch dressing homemade, or store bought
8 ounces cream cheese

TOPPINGS:
1/4 cup sliced olives optional
6 sliced green onions
1/2 cup cilantro fresh, optional
1 avocado optional
1 cup cheddar cheese
1 cup sour cream

INSTRUCTIONS

1. Melt butter in the bottom of a small stock pot or in the instant pot on saute mode, medium heat. As the butter melts, peel and chop the onion, then add to the melted butter. Stir onions occasionally, and when they start to become translucent, add the ground beef and taco seasoning.

2. Brown ground beef, then add in the diced tomatoes. Stir in the broth and mix well. Simmer 20-30 minutes.

3. Stir in the ranch dressing and cream cheese and allow cream cheese to melt, another 5 minutes. Add salt and pepper to taste.

4. Serve, garnishing with cheddar cheese, sour cream, sliced green onions, olives, cilantro, and avocado.

 GAPS Notes: *Replace cream cheese with yogurt cheese, use homemade 24-hour sour cream.*

Nutrition per 1/10 recipe: Calories 575 Fat 49g Carbohydrates 10g
Fiber 2g Protein 23g
Net Carbs: 8 grams per serving

DAIRY-FREE TACO SOUP

This taco soup is so yummy and fast to put together! It uses pre-made ranch dressing, or you can make your own.

If using the Instant Pot, this taco soup is a fantastic use of stew meat.

Servings: 10 Net Carbs: 7 Grams per serving

1 tablespoon bacon fat or avocado oil, ghee, or other fat
1 onion
2 pounds ground beef or stew meat cut into bite-sized pieces
3 tablespoons taco seasoning
2 14-ounce cans diced tomatoes
4 cups chicken broth
3/4 cup ranch dressing

TOPPINGS:
1/4 cup sliced olives
6 sliced green onions, white and light green parts only
1/2 cup cilantro, fresh
1 avocado

INSTRUCTIONS

In the Instant Pot on saute mode, medium heat, heat the bacon fat or other fat. As the fat heats, peel and chop the onion, then add to the hot fat. Stir onion occasionally, and when it starts to become translucent, add the beef and taco seasoning.

2. If using Ground beef: Brown ground beef, then add in the diced tomatoes. Stir in the broth and mix well. No need to cook on high pressure if using ground beef.
3. If using Stew Meat: Cook on high pressure for 45 minutes if using stew meat.
4. After cooking the stew meat, tomatoes, and taco seasoning under pressure, return to saute-medium and add in the broth. Simmer over medium heat for 20 minutes.
5. Stir in the ranch dressing, or reserve and add at the table. Add salt and pepper to taste.
6. Serve, garnishing with sliced green onions, olives, cilantro, and avocado.

STEW MEAT AND THE INSTANT POT

The Instant Pot and stew meat are a match made in heaven. The high pressure quickly transforms even a block of frozen stew meat into tender flavorful melt-in-your-mouth goodness. If you are on a beef subscription program like I am, you may have accumulated a few blocks of stew meat in your freezer, unsure about what to do with them.

You certainly can make actual stew with it, but the meat also lends itself to Mexican dishes, like this soup, really well.

Nutrition: Calories 506 Fat 41g Carbohydrates 9g Fiber 2g Protein 23g

SIMPLE HEARTY BEEF STEW

Growing up we never had stew, so I didn't realize how comforting, delicious, and hearty stew was until my 20s. Stew made with inexpensive cuts of beef and vegetables stretches the budget, while the high pressure of the Instant Pot or long cooking time of the slow cooker tenderizes otherwise tough meat. The tomato base pulls the whole stew together.

While you can use your Instant Pot for many things, it's really excels at making a delicious stew.

The chunky vegetables give this stew color, flavor, and structure- we opted to omit any thickener (traditionally corn starch) to keep this hearty paleo stew allergy-friendly and super easy to prepare.

Prep Time: 25 Minutes Cook Time: 45 minutes (Instant Pot) 8 hours (Slow Cooker) Servings: 6

2 pounds stew meat cut into 1-inch cubes

1 tablespoon tallow or other cooking fat

1/2 teaspoon freshly ground black pepper

1-1/2 teaspoons sea salt

2 large onions chopped into one-inch pieces

3 large carrots scrubbed and chopped into one-inch pieces

6 stalks celery scrubbed and chopped into one-inch pieces

1 six-ounce can tomato paste

2 cups homemade chicken or beef broth unsalted

1 tablespoon apple cider vinegar

INSTRUCTIONS

1.   Heat Instant Pot to Saute - High and melt fat in the bottom.
2.   Once the fat is melted, add beef and sprinkle beef with salt and pepper.
3.   Brown beef on all sides, stirring every 5 minutes or so with a wooden spoon. Beef should be brown in about 15 minutes. Chop your vegetables while you brown the meat.
4.   Add onion, carrots, and celery and stir to mix.
5.   Pour tomato paste, chicken broth, and apple cider vinegar over the top, stirring again with the spoon to mix.
6.   Place lid on Instant Pot and cook on high pressure for 45 minutes.
7.   After cooking, allow pressure to release on its own for the most tender meat, but in a pinch you can usethe quick-release valve.
8.   Serve and enjoy!

To cook in the slow cooker: In a large pan or cast iron skillet over medium-high heat melt fat and brown stew meat on all sides, approxamately 3 minutes per side. Scrape browned meat into the slow cooker. While the pan is still hot, add apple cider vinegar and 1/2 cup of the broth and scrape up all the browned bits with a wooden spatula.

Once the bits have been scraped up, transfer all the liquid to the slow cooker, pouring over the meat. Add in the salt, onions, carrots, celery, tomato paste, and the rest of the broth. Cook on low for 8-10 hours. Add black pepper right before serving.

Nutrition 1/6 recipe:
Calories 347 Fat 14g Carbohydrates 8g Fiber 2g Sugar 3g Protein 43g

SHEPHERD'S PIE SOUP

Shepherd's pie is a much-loved classic. We make it using pureed cauliflower instead of potatoes, but typically it's a layered dish made with seasoned ground lamb, a layer of vegetables such as green beans, and then topped with mashed potatoes, which become a beautiful delicious crust when baked in the oven.

Shepherd's pie soup adds nourishing broth to the recipe, and omits the casserole dish in favor of a soup pot. This soup is a great one to pressure can. After re-heating and mashing the cauliflower, you can add in optional cream cheese and fresh or frozen veggies for a super fast meal that is hearty and delicious.

MAKES 4 SERVINGS

3 tablespoons salted butter
1 large yellow onion
1 pound ground Lamb (ground beef can be used)
2 cups beef broth
1/4 head Cauliflower equal to 1 lbs
1 teaspoon oregano, dried
2 cloves garlic, crushed
1/2 teaspoon mustard powder
1/4 teaspoon ground sage
¾ teaspoon Sea Salt
1 ½ cups mixed frozen vegetables
Salt/Pepper to taste
4 ounces Cream Cheese *Sour cream or heavy cream can be used, or this can be omitted completely*
1/2 cup shredded cheese *optional*

1. In stock pot, melt butter over medium heat. Peel and chop onion. Add to butter and saute until soft, about 10 minutes.
2. When onion is soft, add in lamb and brown, continuing over medium heat. Stir every few minutes, scraping from the bottom. Once lamb is browned, about 15 minutes, set lamb and onions aside.
3. In the same stock pot, with the lamb and onion removed, put in beef stock. Chop and add cauliflower. Cook covered, still over medium heat, until cauliflower is soft, about 5 minutes once it starts simmering.
4. Use an immersion blender or potato masher, mash cauliflower to desired thickness. This thickens the soup and makes it like 'mashed potatoes' without the carbs.
5. Add in the lamb/onions to the mashed cauliflower/broth. Add in the oregano, mustard powder, ground sage, and sea salt. Reduce heat to simmer.
6. Add in the frozen vegetables and simmer until vegetables are hot. Remove from heat and stir in cream cheese. Let sit 3 minutes and then stir again.
7. Serve, adding salt and pepper to taste and optional shredded cheese.

Nutrition (1/4 recipe):
Calories 613 Fat 49g Carbohydrates 16g Fiber 4g Protein 29g

TOMATO MEATBALL SOUP

Makes 4 Servings

This meatball soup is delicious, hearty, and creamy. The meatballs are so good that you may want to double the batch and have some to eat as the soup cooks!

INGREDIENTS

For the Meatballs:
1 egg beaten
¼ cup pork rinds crushed, or crumbs.
3 cloves garlic crushed
1 teaspoon sea salt
½ teaspoon pepper
1 lb. ground beef
1 lb. ground pork
1 Tablespoon olive oil

Time Saving Option:

Use frozen meatballs in place of homemade for time savings.

For the Soup:
1 tablespoon butter
1 yellow onion diced
1 bell pepper diced
3 cloves garlic crushed
2 tablespoons tomato paste
4 cups beef broth
2 14.5 oz. cans diced tomatoes, undrained
1 teaspoon hot sauce (optional)
½ cup heavy cream
2 cups spinach
1 teaspoon dried oregano
1 teaspoon dried basil
1 teaspoon dried parsley
1 teaspoon mustard powder
1 pinch red pepper flakes
Salt/Pepper to taste

For Serving:
8 oz. Ricotta Cheese
½ cup Parmesan Cheese
Red Pepper Flakes

MAKE THE MEATBALLS

1. Whisk the egg in a large bowl with a fork. Add pork rind crumbs, garlic, salt, and pepper and stir to combine. Add the ground beef and ground pork and gently combine with a fork and your hands until the egg mixture is evenly distributed. Don't overwork the meat.
2. Roll the meat mixture into 1-inch balls.
3. Heat the olive oil in a 4 ½ quart stock pot or Dutch oven over medium-high heat.
4. Brown the meatballs in batches for 2-3 minutes, add more olive oil throughout cooking and decrease heat slightly as needed. The inside of the meatballs will finish cooking in the soup.
5. Remove the meatballs and set aside.

MAKE THE SOUP

1. Melt the butter in the same stock pot that you used to brown the meatballs over medium-low heat. Add onions and cook for 10 minutes, a little longer than normal as this will release some of their sugar which counteracts the acidity of the tomatoes. Stir every few minutes.
2. Add the peppers and cook for 4 minutes. Add the garlic, tomato paste, hot sauce, and seasonings. Cook for 1 minute.
3. Add in the broth and tomatoes.
4. Bring to a boil, then reduce to a simmer. Let it simmer uncovered for 15 minutes. You can also simmer it longer to concentrate the flavor and thicken it more.
5. Stir the soup and bring the soup to a gentle boil. Add the meatballs and and return it to a gentle boil.
6. Reduce heat to low and stir in heavy cream, then add the spinach and cook until wilted, about 1 minute.
7. Transfer to serving bowls and top with ricotta cheese, Parmesan, and red pepper flakes.

Nutrition (1/4 recipe) Calories 727 Fat 55g Carbohydrates 21g Fiber 4g Sugar 11g Protein 40g

Net carbs=17g

SPECIAL DIET NOTES:
GAPS: Use coconut milk in place of the cream, omit ricotta.
Paleo: Omit cheese, use coconut milk in place of cream.

HEARTY BEEF-BROCCOLI SOUP

Makes 4 Servings

Broccoli Beef Soup is a warm and filling winter classic, that is rich in protein from the beef chunks and homemade broth. Make use of broccoli and onions during the winter, as they are seasonal, inexpensive, and give a burst of green in an otherwise white winter wonderland.

This soup is mostly made in the slow cooker, with the meat added at the end to preserve texture and flavor. Pack in a thermos for the next day's lunch.

1-2 quarts chicken or beef broth
Filtered water
1.5 pounds beef any cut (tritip pictured)
2 teaspoons sea salt divided
4 cloves garlic
2 onions chopped
2 pounds broccoli florets fresh or frozen
Optional: 1 cup shredded cheddar cheese

SLOW COOKER INSTRUCTIONS

1. In a slow cooker, combine broth, filtered water to fill the slow cooker ¾ full, 1 tablespoon sea salt, garlic, and broccoli. Cover, and allow to cook on low all day.
2. An hour before you are ready to eat, cut beef into ½ inch cubes, season with a pinch of salt and brown in a skillet over medium high heat until browned on the outside and partially cooked.
3. Using an immersion blender, puree the soup in the slow cooker, leaving some chunks of broccoli and onion if desired.
4. Add beef to pureed soup and allow to cook until dinner time.
5. Taste and adjust salt as necessary.
6. Ladle into bowls and top with optional cheese to serve.

INSTANT POT INSTRUCTIONS

1. Cut beef into ½ inch cubes, season with a pinch of salt.
2. Place beef cubes, crushed garlic, and chopped onions in the bottom of the Instant Pot using the saute function on high heat until beef is browned on the outside and partially cooked.
3. Transfer beef to a bowl and set aside, leaving the onions, garlic, and bits from cooking the beef in the bottom of the Instant Pot.
4. Using the same pot that you cooked the beef in and keeping over high heat, add broth, 1 teaspoon sea salt, and broccoli. Bring to a boil and cook 10 minutes, or until broccoli is soft.
5. Using an immersion blender, puree the soup in the slow cooker, leaving some chunks of broccoli and onion if desired.
6. Add beef to pureed soup and allow to cook until dinner time.
7. Add salt to taste and top with cheddar cheese if desired. Enjoy!

Nutition: Calories 403 Fat 24g Carbohydrates 20g
Fiber 6g Protein 33g

PHILLY CHEESESTEAK SOUP

This Philly Cheesesteak Soup is so delicious, and it's easy and fun to make! The provolone cheese melts over top of the bowl, making the soup a surprise underneath a creamy layer of cheese.

This soup is fantastically low carb with only 7 grams net carbs per hearty serving.

Makes 8 Servings

12 tablespoons butter, olive oil, or other cooking fat
2 onions
2 green bell peppers
2 pounds beef skirt steak (or ribeye)
2 cloves garlic crushed
1 teaspoon sea salt only if your broth is unsalted
1/4 cup red wine or some of the broth
3 cups beef broth
2 cups water
8 ounces provolone cheese

INSTRUCTIONS

1. Heat butter in a large saucepan over medium heat and saute onions and bell pepper slices.
2. Cut up beef as vegetables cook. Thinly slice beef, cutting across the grain in 1/8 inch slices.
3. Remove vegetables and add in beef, garlic and salt. Cook, 5 mins. Remove meat and deglaze pan with red wine or broth. Add beef, onions and peppers back in. Add in broth and water. Simmer, covered, for 30 minutes.
4. Ladle into bowls and top each bowl with a slice of provolone. Allow provolone to melt for 2-3 minutes before serving.

Nutrition (1/8 recipe): Calories 506 Fat 41g Carbohydrates 9 Fiber 2g Protein 23g

LOW CARB BROCCOLI HAM AND CHEESE SOUP

This rich soup is a delicious warming meal in a bowl. With bright broccoli, creamy cheese, hearty ham, and nourishing broth, you're going to be set for whatever cold weather comes your way!

Makes: 6 servings

5 pieces bacon, cut into 1-inch slices
1 onion, white or yellow
3 cloves garlic minced or crushed
3 cups chicken broth
3 cups broccoli (approx 12 oz)
2 ounces cream cheese
1.5 cups cream heavy cream
3 cups chopped ham (approx 12 oz)
1/4 teaspoon nutmeg
1 teaspoon sea salt, to taste
1/2 teaspoon black pepper, to taste
2 cups cheddar cheese grated; plus an additional cup to garnish if desired
1/4 teaspoon Xanthan gum optional, but helps thicken

1. In a stock pot over medium heat, cook bacon until crisp. As the bacon cooks, chop onion.
2. Once crisp, set bacon aside, leaving grease in the pot. Add chopped onion and crushed garlic to bacon grease on medium heat. Saute until the onion is soft, about 10 minutes.
3. Add in the broth, broccoli, and spices and bring to a simmer. Simmer for 10 minutes.
4. Reduce heat to low and wait for bubbles to stop. Add in the cream and ham.
5. Slowly add in cheese 1/4 cup at a time, stirring continually, still over low heat.
6. If using Xanthan gum, sprinkle over the top after all the cheese is added, allow xanthan gum to sit for 1 minute, and then stir in.
7. Serve soup and top with cooked bacon and optional extra shredded cheese. Enjoy!
8. Leftovers can be kept covered in the fridge for up to 1 week

Nutrition (1/6 recipe): Calories 575 Fat 50g Carbohydrates 7g
Fiber 1g Sugar 1g Protein 26g
Net carbs=6g

GAPS Notes: Make sure bacon and ham are sugar-free, use yogurt cheese in place of cream cheese, use coconut milk or cultured cream in place of heavy cream, omit Xanthan gum.

RICH AND CREAMY PUMPKIN SAUSAGE SOUP

This pumpkin soup is another weekly soup all winter long. The sausage makes it a full meal, and the pumpkin gives a creamy thick base without using a traditional thickener such as flour. Using canned pumpkin and canned coconut milk makes this soup so fast to whip up, a welcome break for those of us who normally cook everything from scratch.

Makes: 6 Servings. Prep time: 15 min. Cook time: 20-30 min.

2 slices bacon or 1 tablespoon bacon fat
1 pound pork sausage uncooked
1 onion diced
2 garlic cloves crushed
1 tablespoon italian seasoning
1/2 teaspoon red pepper flakes optional
1/2 teaspoon sea salt plus more to taste
1 15-ounce can pumpkin
4 cups chicken broth
1 cup heavy cream or 1 can coconut milk
1 cup water

1. Fry 2 slices of bacon in the bottom of a small stock pot or in the instant pot on saute mode, medium heat. Once crisp, remove and reserve to garnish soup at the end.
2. Brown sausage, drain.
3. To the browned sausage, add the onion, garlic, Italian seasoning and optional red pepper flakes, and sea salt, and sauté until done.
4. Add pumpkin to this mixture and mix well.
5. Stir in the broth and mix well.
6. Simmer 20-30 minutes.
7. Stir in half of the the heavy cream or coconut milk and water and simmer on low another 10-15 minutes. Add salt and pepper to taste.
8. Serve, garnishing with remaining cream or coconut milk and topping with optional crumbled bacon.

Flavor Tip: This soup can be made into curry flavor by omitting the italian seasoning and adding in 1 inch of grated fresh ginger and an additional clove of crushed garlic, 1/2 teaspoon curry powder if desired.

Calories 440 Fat 38g Carbohydrates 10g Fiber 2g Protein 14g
Net carbs= 8g

HEALTH HOME & HAPPINESS

CHICKEN AND POULTRY SOUPS

Chicken soup is good for the soul... and gut, and skin, and, well, everything! Chicken and poultry are delicious with so many flavors, giving lots of variety and a little less 'heaviness' than soup made with red meat.

From Classic Chicken and Vegetable to Zesty Greek Lemon Chicken to Low Carb Turkey Pot Pie Soup, you're going to love these recipes!

Chicken & Poultry Soups

WHITE CHICKEN CHILI

A delicious change of pace from red chili, White Chicken Chili is beautiful and easy to make with pre-cooked chicken. The beans stretch the budget, but they also add carbs. Omit beans if needed for preference or dietary needs.

MAKES 8 SERVINGS

2 tablespoons butter or ghee
1 whole medium onion diced
4 cloves garlic crushed
2 Anaheim chilis seeds removed, diced
1 whole Jalapeno Sliced
1 pound white navy beans, soaked overnight and drained
4 cups chicken broth
4 cups filtered water
1½ teaspoons ground cumin
½ teaspoon paprika

½ teaspoon cayenne pepper
1 teaspoon sea salt, more to taste
1 cup heavy cream or half and half
1/8 teaspoon xanthan gum to thicken
3 cups cooked chicken diced
½ pound grated Monterey Jack cheese
Plain yogurt or sour cream for garnish
Guacamole or sliced avocado for garnish

PREP STEP: Soak Beans

Rinse navy beans in a colander, removing any rocks or debris that may be in the package.

Place beans in a large bowl (they will swell to triple their current size) and cover with filtered water so that they are covered by an inch or more. Allow to soak for 24 hours, changing the water once during this timeperiod.

This reduces the starch content of the beans and makes them easier to digest.

MAKE THE SOUP

Stovetop Directions:

1. In a large pot over medium heat cook the onion and garlic in butter until soft.
2. Sprinkle xantham gum over onion and garlic and mix gently. This will thicken the chili (GAPS diet adaptation- see note)
3. Add in the diced chili, and jalapeno and cook until soft, 5 minutes.
4. Add the navy beans, chicken broth, filtered water, cumin, paprika, cayenne pepper, and sea salt.
5. Cook in the slow cooker all day on low, or 4 hours on high.
6. After the beans are cooked through, 20-30 minutes before serving, stir in the chicken.
7. Stir in cream.
8. Add Monterey Jack cheese to the pot just before serving and stir to melt.

Instant Pot Directions:

1. Heat the Instant Pot to Saute-medium and cook the onion and garlic in butter until soft.
2. Sprinkle xantham gum over onion and garlic and mix gently. This will thicken the chili (GAPS diet adaptation- see note)
3. Add in the diced chili, and jalapeno and cook until soft, 5 minutes.
4. Add the navy beans, chicken broth, filtered water, cumin, paprika, cayenne pepper, and sea salt.
5. Place lid on Instant Pot and turn to lock.
6. Cook on manual- high pressure- for 45 minutes
7. After the 45 minutes is up, allow pressure to come down manually.
8. Remove lid and set to saute - low
9. Stir in the chicken.

10. Mix in the cream.
11. Add Monterey Jack cheese to the pot just before serving and stir to melt.

Slow Cooker   Directions:

1. In a skillet over medium heat cook the onion and garlic in butter until soft.
2. Sprinkle xantham gum over onion and garlic and mix gently. This will thicken the chili (GAPS diet adaptation- see note below)
3. Add in the diced chili, and jalapeno and cook until soft, 5 minutes.
4. Scrape everything from the skillet into the slow cooker.
5. Add the navy beans, chicken broth, filtered water, cumin, paprika, cayenne pepper, and sea salt.
6. Cook in the slow cooker all day on low, or 4 hours on high.
7. After the beans are cooked through, 20-30 minutes before serving, stir in the chicken.
8. Mix in the cream.
9. Add Monterey Jack cheese to the pot just before serving and stir to melt.

Nutrition:
Fat 22g Carbohydrates 39g Fiber 14g Protein 34g

Net carbs: 25 net carbs

SPECIAL DIET NOTES:

GAPS Diet: Use 24-hour yogurt in place of the cream, omit xanthan gum and instead whisk 2 egg yolks into the yogurt before adding. This will thicken your chili.

CLASSIC CHICKEN & VEGETABLE SOUP

Classic recipe, nourishing ingredients. This recipe is easily adaptable for any vegetable that you have on hand.

MAKES 5 SERVINGS

2 tablespoons chicken fat, butter, or ghee
4 cloves garlic
1 medium yellow onion
2 pounds boneless chicken thighs
4 stalks celery
3 large carrots
1 tablespoon apple cider vinegar
1 quart chicken stock
2 cups water
1 teaspoon sea salt
1/2 teaspoon dried sage
1/4 teaspoon dried thyme
Additional salt if needed
1/4 teaspoon freshly ground black pepper

1. In a stock pot, melt fat over medium heat.
2. As the fat melts, prepare garlic and onion. Crush garlic, and add to the melted butter. Peel and dice onion, and add to the melted fat. Lower heat to medium-low and stir occasionally, about 10 minutes, until onion is translucent.
3. As the onions and garlic cook, prepare chicken by patting dry and cutting into 1-inch cubes.
4. Add chicken to the fat, garlic, and onions. Raise the heat to medium, and cook chicken in the pot until cooked through and edges are golden, about 5 minutes on each side for a total of 20 minutes. As the chicken cooks, begin washing and chopping veggies.
5. Wash and cut the celery into 1/4 inch ribs. Peel carrots and cut into 1/4-inch thick rounds. Peel winter squash and cut into 1/2-inch cubes. Rinse tomatoes and halve if desired.
6. Use a spatula or slotted spoon to remove chicken to a bowl or glass container. Leave most of the garlic and onion in the pot, it's okay if a little comes with the chicken though.

7. Set chicken aside, cover, and transfer to the fridge. We will add the chicken back in after the vegetables in the soup cooks to keep the chicken from drying out and losing flavor.
8. Add whatever veggies you have chopped to the pot after removing the chicken, and continue chopping veggies, scraping the bottom of the pot and turning veggies with each addition.
9. Once all veggies are added, add in chicken broth, water, and sea salt.
10. Increase heat to medium until simmering, then cover the pot and lower the heat down to a low simmer.
11. Simmer for at least one hour, until winter squash and carrots are very soft.
12. Add chicken back in 15 minutes before serving, and add salt and freshly ground black pepper to taste.

Nutrition information: Calories 544 Fat 38g Carbohydrates 15g Fiber 2g Protein 35g

Net carbs: 13 g per serving

FLAVOR ADAPTATIONS

In place of the sage and thyme, make a warming soup by substituting 1/2 teaspoon dried ginger and adding a dash of red pepper flakes.

Add any of the following to dress up this classic soup:

- Parmesan cheese
- Grated cheddar cheese
- Soy Sauce or Coconut Aminos
- Hot Sauce
- Sour Cream
- Fresh sage, thinly sliced
- A squeeze of fresh lemon juice

USE-WHAT-YOU-HAVE SOUP FORUMLA

As you have been making soup, you see how easily different flavors can meld into a delicious soup. As you've gained confidence, you can use this formula to start to improvise.

This soup formula is perfect for the day before grocery shopping day, when you're stuck inside due to bad weather, or any time the grocery money isn't stretching as far as you'd like it to!

Step 1. Fat and aromatics: Heat your stock pot or Instant Pot (saute) to medium heat. Melt 1/4 cup of your fat of choice (bacon fat, beef fat, butter, olive oil) and then stir in 1 chopped onion or a few cloves crushed garlic and saute. As these saute move onto step 2.

Step 2. Veggie Base: Wash and chop into bite-sized pieces any hearty veggies you have in the fridge and add to the fat and aromatics you started in step 1, continuing over medium heat: Winter squash, carrots, celery, celery root, green beans, beets, onions, peppers, etc.

Do not include anything that will turn bitter or off tasting with a long cooking time: Leafy greens, broccoli, cauliflower, peas, etc.

Step 3. Season
- Add in salt (start with 1 teaspoon and go up from there 1/4 teaspoon at a time).
- Add black pepper, starting with 1/4 teaspoon.
- Add 1 tablepoon of acid: Apple cider vinegar, red wine, or lemon juice. This makes the flavors pop.
- Optional: Add 1 teaspoon dried herbs: I love sage and often add it.

Step 4: Broth. Add broth (or a combination of broth and water) to cover the vegetables in the stock pot. Bring broth to a simmer, and then lower to medium-low and simmer, covered, until the vegetables are tender, about 30 minutes.

Step 5: Add in leftover cooked protein that you need to use up. Cube: Leftover chicken, steak, seafood, or a combination of any meat. Cooked beans can be added as well. Heat until protein is cooked through, about 15 minutes.

Step 6: Top and Serve! Top with any garnish you have; shredded cheese, fresh herbs, pumpkin seeds, balsamic vinegar- less is more, but a little something really dresses up the soup!

AUTUMN VEGETABLE SOUP WITH CHICKEN

Classic recipe, nourishing ingredients. This recipe is easily adaptable for any vegetable that you have on hand.

Makes 6 Servings

2 tablespoons chicken fat, butter, or ghee
4 cloves garlic
3 medium yellow onions
2 pounds boneless chicken thighs
3 large carrots
1 butternut squash or buttercup squash
1 quart chicken broth
2 cup water
1 inch fresh garlic, peeled and grated or diced
1 teaspoon sea salt

Additional salt if needed
1/4 teaspoon freshly ground black pepper

1. In a stock pot, melt fat over medium heat.
2. As the fat melts, prepare garlic and onion. Crush garlic, and add to the melted butter. Peel and dice onion, and add to the melted fat. Lower heat to medium-low and stir occasionally, about 10 minutes, until onion is translucent.
3. As the onions and garlic cook, prepare chicken by patting dry and cutting into 1-inch cubes. Add to the fat, garlic, and onions. Raise the heat to medium, and cook chicken in the pot until cooked through and edges are golden, about 5 minutes on each side for a total of 20 minutes. As the chicken cooks, begin washing and chopping veggies.
4. Wash and cut the celery into 1/4 inch ribs. Peel carrots and cut into 1/4-inch thick rounds. Peel winter squash and cut into 1/2-inch cubes. Rinse tomatoes and halve if desired. Cut cabbage into thin long strips as vegetable 'noodles'.
5. Use a spatula or slotted spoon to remove chicken to a bowl or glass container. Leave most of the garlic and onion in the pot, it's okay if a little comes with the chicken though. Set chicken aside, cover, and transfer to the fridge. We will add the chicken back in after the vegetables in the soup cooks to keep the chicken from drying out and losing flavor.
6. Add whatever veggies you have chopped to the pot after removing the chicken, and continue chopping veggies, scraping the bottom of the pot and turning veggies with each addition. Once all veggies are chopped and added, add in chicken stock, water, and sea salt. Increase heat to medium until simmering, then cover the pot and lower the heat down to a low simmer. Simmer for at least one hour, until winter squash and carrots are very soft.
7. Add chicken back in 15 minutes before serving, and add salt and freshly ground black pepper to taste.

Tip: This is a nourishing and sinus-clearning soup that is perfect when you are feeling under the weather.

Nutrition (1/6 recipe): Calories 521 Fat 32g Carbohydrates 30g
Fiber 4g Protein 31g
Net carbs=26 g

ZESTY GREEK LEMON-CHICKEN SOUP

Full of bright light flavor, Greek Lemon-Chicken Soup is topped with feta and chives and brings a lighter flavor, with all the nutrition to your table this winter. This soup is a great way to use up meat you have accumulated while making chicken stock, or you just use boneless skinless chicken breasts or thighs.

Makes: 6 Servings

2 tablespoons olive oil

1 onion peeled, cut in half, and cut into thin half-rings

6 cloves garlic crushed or minced

4 cups chicken broth

2 cups filtered water

1-2 lbs boneless-skinless chicken breast or thigh

1 lemon juiced and zested

1/2 teaspoon red pepper flakes

1 teaspoon sea salt or to taste

1/2 teaspoon freshly-ground black pepper or to taste

1 bunch fresh chives

2 ounces feta cheese crumbled

INSTRUCTIONS

1. In the bottom of a stock pot or using the saute function of the Instant Pot, heat olive oil (can also use avocado oil) over medium heat and add onion.
2. Saute onions in oil until soft, about 10 minutes.
3. Keeping the heat on, add garlic, chicken broth, filtered water, skinless chicken breast or thighs (whole, we will shred it in another step), lemon zest and juice, red pepper flakes, salt, and pepper.
4. Once the soup is simmering, lower heat to medium-low (or low on the Instant Pot Saute Function) and cook an additional 30 minutes, or until chicken is cooked through when pierced with a knife. If you need the soup to be done faster, use the pressure setting on the pressure cooker- Manual for 10 minutes with the lid on and set to Seal.
5. Remove the chicken and shred with 2 forks on a plate or cutting board, and return to the soup. Taste and add red pepper flakes, black pepper, or salt as desired.
6. To serve, ladle soup into bowls. Top with snipped chives and crumbled feta. Enjoy!

Nutrition (1/6 recipe): Calories 227 Fat 10g Carbohydrates 10g Fiber 3g Sugar 4g Protein 22g Net carbs= 7 g

> ### Time Saving Tip:
>
> Use rotisserie chicken in place of raw to make this soup super fast!

CREAMY LOW-CARB TURKEY POT PIE SOUP

This creamy soup is loaded with leftover turkey and classic veggies. You can adapt this soup to be lower carb, and even dairy free!

Makes 4 servings

FOR THE CREAMY CAULIFLOWER BASE:
4 cups 16 ounces cauliflower florets

2 cloves garlic

3 cups turkey broth beef or chicken broth also work

3/4 teaspoon salt more or less to taste

FOR THE REST OF THE SOUP:
1 cup sliced carrots frozen is fine

1 cup pearl onions frozen is fine

16 ounce cooked turkey cubed (16 ounce = approx 3 cups)

1/2 teaspoon sage

1/2 cup heavy cream optional

1/2 cup frozen peas

1/4 cup parmesan cheese optional

FOR THE CAULIFLOWER BASE
1. In a stock pot, add cauliflower, garlic, salt, and broth. The garlic doesn't have to be crushed- we'll mash it in the next step. Cook on medium, covered, for 10 minutes, or until cauliflower is tender.
2. Using an immersion blender or a potato masher, blend/mash cauliflower and garlic, until it as smooth as desired.

FOR THE REST OF THE SOUP:
1. To the pureed cauliflower and broth, add carrots, onions, turkey, and sage. Continue cooking over medium heat for 5-10 minutes, until heated through.
2. Add in the cream and parmesan if using, and stir. Add the peas last (over cooked peas are never good) and then serve.

Calories 439 Fat 22g Carbohydrates 24g Fiber 11g Protein 38g

Net-carbs: 13g per serving

DAIRY FREE To make this recipe dairy-free, use coconut milk in place of the heavy cream, or omit completely and just have the cauliflower base as a creamy base. Omit parmesan cheese and sprinkle with nutritional yeast for a similar flavor if desired.

RANCH CHICKEN SOUP

Ranch dressing flavors + hearty chicken and bacon, what more could you want in a meal? To make it even faster (though this recipe is really fast as written) use rotisserie chicken. Don't forget to save the carcass (bones) to make broth with!

Makes 6 servings

1 pound bacon

1 onion

4 cloves garlic

2 pounds chicken breasts

1 teaspoon sea salt (omit if using salted broth)

2 blocks cream cheese

4 cloves garlic

4 cups chicken broth

1 teaspoon chives dried or 1 tablespoon fresh

1 teaspoon parsley dried or 1 tablespoon fresh

1. Cook bacon in an Instant Pot on Saute mode, medium, until crisp. Remove bacon and set aside, leaving drippings in the bottom of the Instant Pot.
2. Leaving the Instant Pot set to Saute-Medium cook the onions for 5 minutes, until they start to soften. Add crushed garlic and cook another 2 minutes, stirring with a spatula a couple times.
3. Set cooked onions and garlic aside to add in a couple minutes.
4. Remove onions, place chicken in the bottom of the instant pot, cover with salt and chives, then add onions to the top. Pour chicken broth over the top.
5. Cook at high pressure for 45 minutes then let pressure release naturally.
6. Use 2 forks to shred the chicken.
7. Cube cream cheese and stir into shredded chicken. Serve the soup into bowls.
8. Top each bowl with grated sharp cheddar, sliced green onions, and bacon that you cooked in the first step.

SERVING SUGGESTION

This soup is rich and hearty, serve with a light steamed veggie such as broccoli, cauliflower, or snow peas for a side, or just on its own.

CHICKEN CORDON BLEU SOUP

The flavors and creamy texture of this soup make it a real comfort food, and it's a fast one perfect for a quick hearty meal too! Leftovers are even more yummy the next day, just be careful not to bring it to a boil when reheating so the cream doesn't turn grainy.

Makes 4 servings

4 tablespoons butter, ghee, or olive oil
1/2 large onion chopped
2 carrots chopped
2 stalks celery chopped
4 garlic cloves minced
1/4 teaspoon Xanthan gum (optional, to thicken the soup)
6 cups chicken broth
2 cups half and half
2 cups cooked and cubed ham
2 cups shredded chicken, cooked
3 tablespoons Dijon mustard
1 teaspoon dried parsley or 1 tablespoon fresh
1/2 teaspoon dried oregano,
1/2 teaspoon dried thyme
1/4 tsp red pepper flakes

2 cups (8 oz.) Swiss cheese shredded
Salt and black pepper to taste
Sprig of fresh thyme for garnish, optional

Directions:

1. In a stock pot or Instant Pot using the Saute function, melt butter over medium heat. Add chopped onions and cook until soft, about 10 minutes.
2. Add in chopped carrots, celery, garlic, and optional Xanthan gum and cook an additional 5 minutes, stirring occasionally and scraping the bottom of the pan as you stir.
3. Add in broth and bring up to a boil. Turn down to simmer and cook, covered, for about 10 minutes or until carrots are soft.
4. Turn heat down to medium low and add in the half and half, cubed ham, shredded chicken, dijon mustard, parsley, oregano, and red pepper flakes. Heat until half and half is warm, about 10 minutes.
5. 5 minutes before serving stir in swiss cheese, about 1/4 cup at a time, reserving some for garnish if desired. Add salt and pepper to taste, serve, and enjoy!

Nutrition: Calories 810 Fat 60g
Carbohydrates 14g Fiber 2g Protein 54g

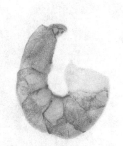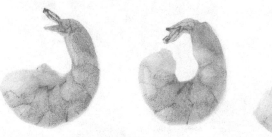

Fish and seafood soups are absolutely delicious, and a great way to include nturient-dense seafood. When you bone and skin fish, or shell shrimp or other seafood, make sure you save all these pieces for delicate seafood broth.

The recipes in this section are really good using seafood broth, but feel free to use chicken or beef broth, they both go well with fish and seafood as well.

Fish soups are quick to make since fish cooks so quickly. The different flavors in these soups are sure to be a hit!

Once a week seafood for the omega 3 fatty acids is a great goal, and these soups make delicious meals out of this yummy and nutrient-dense food.

Fish and Seafood Soups

Seafood and Eyesight

Move on over carrots! If you want to help your eyes, fish and seafood may be the answer. The high amount of omega 3 fatty acids as well as zinc in seafood are thought to be incredably important in the development and continued health of the eye.

Aim for 4 ounces of seafood at least once a week for children (including babies once food has been introduced around 6 months) and adults for help not only with eyesight, but in whole body health.

Don't want to eat seafood? It may sound old fashioned, but there is timelss benefit in taking a teaspoon of cod liver oil a day!

Fish Broth Recipe

Like all broths, fish broth is adaptable to what you have on hand. It is more delicate and requires less cooking time than beef or chicken broth.

1 cup bone-in fish parts (heads, bones pulled from fish, or whole fish including scales and bones)
2 quarts filtered water
1 teaspoon sea salt

Instructions: In the Instant Pot on Saute or in a stock pot over medium heat, combine the fish parts, water, and sea salt. Once the water starts to boil, about 20 minutes, reduce heat to medium-low and simmer for 60 minutes. Remove from heat and skim the surface of the broth to remove any impurities that rose to the surface.

Pour broth through a fine sieve and store in the refridgerator, covered, for 1 week or in the freezer for 1 year. Can also be canned following the directions for canning broth on page 80.

MEDITERRANEAN SEAFOOD SOUP

8 oz Sea Scallops

Salt and black pepper

Butter, bacon grease, or olive oil

1 ½ lb shrimp peeled and deveined

1 green bell pepper cored, chopped

1 red bell pepper cored, chopped

1 medium yellow onion chopped

6 garlic cloves peeled, minced

3 tbsp tomato paste

1 tbsp dried oregano divided

7 cups fish broth (page 51)

3 large tomatoes diced (canned diced tomato will work as well)

6 oz baby spinach

1 cup chopped fresh parsley leaves

1 cup chopped fresh dill stems removed

1 lemon, juiced

Crushed red pepper flakes *optional*

1. Pat scallops dry and season with salt and pepper.
2. In a stock pot, heat 1 tablespoon butter, bacon grease, or olive oil over medium-high heat until shimmering. Gently add the sea scallops. Sear for about 1 ½ minutes on each side. Scallops should form a golden brown crust. Sprinkle a large pinch of dried oregano. Transfer to a dish and set aside.
3. To the same stock pot, add a little more butter if needed. Again heat over medium-high. Add the shrimp; sear for about 2 minutes on both sides. You want to see some pink, but don't worry about fully cooking it (you will finish cooking it in the soup.) Remove from the heat and sprinkle a generous pinch of dried oregano.
4. In the same stock pot, heat another tablespoon of butter.. Add the chopped peppers, onions, garlic, tomato paste, salt and the remaining dried oregano. Cook for 5 minutes, stirring occasionally.
5. Add the broth and bring to a boil. Add the diced tomatoes. Cook on medium-high for 3-5 more minutes.
6. Stir in the baby spinach, parsley, dill, and lemon juice.
7. Finally, stir in the scallops and shrimp to warm through (about 1 to 2 minutes.) Taste and adjust seasoning to taste. Add crushed red pepper flakes for some heat, if you like.

Nutrition: Calories 325 Fat 4g Carbohydrates 24g Fiber 5g Protein 53g Net carbs= 19

DAIRY FREE

THAI SHRIMP SOUP

This soup is creamy, fresh, and delicious! It's fast too, you'll love this soup!

Makes 4 Servings

2 tablespoons butter
1 pound shrimp, peeled and deveined
Sea salt and freshly ground black pepper to taste
2 cloves garlic minced
1 onion diced
1 red bell pepper diced
1 tablespoon ginger root, peeled and grated
2 tablespoon red curry paste
12 ounces unsweetened coconut milk (*one standard can = 12 ounces*)
3 cups fish broth (page 51)
1 lime Juiced
2 tablespoons chopped fresh cilantro leaves

1. Melt butter in a large stockpot or Dutch oven over medium high heat. Add shrimp, salt and pepper, to taste. Cook, stirring occasionally, until pink, about 2-3 minutes; set aside.
2. Add garlic, onion and bell pepper to the stockpot. Cook, stirring occasionally, until tender, about 3-4 minutes. Stir in ginger until fragrant, about 1 minute.
3. Whisk in curry paste until well combined, about 1 minute. Gradually whisk in coconut milk and broth, and cook, whisking constantly, until incorporated, about 1-2 minutes.
4. Bring to a boil; reduce heat and simmer until slightly thickened, about 8-10 minutes.
5. Stir in shrimp, lime juice and cilantro.
6. Serve immediately. Garnish with extra cilantro and drizzled coconut milk if desired.

Nutrition (1/4 recipe):
Calories 391 Fat 28g Carbohydrates 12g Fiber 4g Protein 28g
Net carbs: 8g

DAIRY FREE

COD STEW

Clam juice really makes this stew all come together. It may be a new item to add to your cart but it's in the majority of grocery stores. Give it a try, you'll like it! If you prefer to avoid bottled ingredients like this, a shellfish broth works in its place.

6 tablespoons ghee or olive oil
1 medium onion, chopped
3 large cloves garlic, minced
2/3 cup fresh parsley leaves, chopped
1 1/2 cups fresh chopped tomato OR 1 (14-ounce) can whole or crushed tomatoes with their juices
2 teaspoons tomato paste, optional
1 (8-ounce) bottle clam juice or 2 cups fish broth (page 51)
1/2 cup dry white wine (such as Sauvignon blanc)
1 1/2 pounds firm white fish fillets such as halibut or cod, cut into pieces
Pinch dried oregano
Pinch dried thyme
1/8 teaspoon Tabasco sauce , or more to taste
1/8 teaspoon freshly ground black pepper, plus more to taste
1 teaspoon salt, plus more to taste

1. Saute the aromatics in olive oil:
2. Heat olive oil in a large, thick-bottomed pot over medium-high heat. Add onion and sauté 4 minutes. Add the garlic and cook a minute more. Add parsley and stir 2 minutes. Add tomato and tomato paste, and gently cook for 10 more minutes or so.
3. Sauteeing onions in a pot to make a fish soup recipe.
4. Adding chopped tomato and parsley to a pot to make a seafood stew.
5. Sauteeing ingredients to make a seafood stew recipe.
6. Finish the soup:
7. Add clam juice, dry white wine, and fish. Bring to a simmer, and let simmer until the fish is cooked through and easily flakes apart, about 3 to 5 minutes. Add seasoning — salt, pepper, oregano, thyme, and Tabasco. Add more salt and pepper to taste.
8. Ladle into individual bowls and serve.

Nutrition:
Calories 411 Fat 23g Carbohydrates 15g Fiber 2g Protein 32g

Net Carbs: 13 g per 1/4 recipe

DAIRY FREE

SALMON CHOWDER

This rich and hearty dairy-free salmon chowder uses the finest wild-caught salmon with lots of hearty winter vegetables for nutrient-dense chowder. We made it rich in healthy fats that keep our body running smoothly and allow for the absorption of all the needed nutrients in the fish and vegetables by using coconut milk.

Surprisingly, the coconut milk is barely detectible in this soup- coconut tends to give lots of flavor to recipes, but salmon gives even MORE flavor, making this dairy-free chowder perfect for those who usually aren't fans of coconut.

This soup can be made ahead, and reheated when it's time to serve.

1 tablespoon bacon fat or 2 slices bacon, chopped
3/4 lb wild-caught salmon, raw with bones removed or canned
1/2 head cauliflower
1 celery root
2 large carrots
4 stalks celery
1 medium leek
2 cups fish broth (page 51)
1 can full fat coconut milk
1 teaspoon sea salt
1/4 teaspoon cayenne or red pepper flakes
1 bay leaf
4 sprigs fresh thyme

INSTRUCTIONS

1. In the bottom of a large saucepan over medium heat, melt bacon fat or chop bacon into 1/2 inch slices and cook until crispy.
2. While the bacon cooks, cut cauliflower into 1/2-inch pieces, peel and cut celery root into 1/2 inch cubes, cut carrots and celery stalks into small pieces and add to bacon fat and optional bacon, stirring with a wooden spoon or spatula occasionally to prevent burning.
3. Cut both ends off the leek, rinse, and cut the white and light green part into thin rounds. Add to the vegetable mixture.
4. After all the vegetables are chopped, add broth, coconut milk, sea salt, cayenne pepper, and bay leaf. Reduce heat to medium-low and simmer for 10 minutes, or until cauliflower is easily pierced with a fork.
5. Add salmon to the soup and cook for another 10-15 minutes, covered, or until salmon is cooked through and can be flaked easily with a fork. Break up salmon.
6. Serve, topping with the leaves of fresh thyme.

Nutrition: Calories 310 Fat 20g Carbohydrates 15g Fiber 3g Protein 17g

DAIRY FREE

HEARTY LEGUMES: BEANS AND LENTILS

Dried beans are a frugal cook's dream- easy to store, inexpensive, full of protein, and so adaptable! Some people may find that they are sensitive to beans, which is why they are not included on the paleo diet.

If you have felt gassy and bloated from beans before, but want to give them another chance, be sure to follow the steps included in the following recipes for soaking overnight prior to cooking, or even sprouting as directed in the GAPS Notes on the following page.

This soaking not only makes the beans cook much faster, but it also reduces the anti-nutrients in beans and makes them easier to digest, which lessens or totally eliminates gassiness.

When we use beans as our protein source, and also cook them in nutrient-dense broth, we are getting a double whammy of frugal nutrition.

Home Canned Beans:

Canning beans yourself makes these soups and many other bean dishes quick, easy, and also more nutrient dense than store-canned beans. By using the amount of salt and the kind of salt we want, along with broth as our cooking liquid, we are able to pack tons of nutrition into little glass jars, and can them with our pressure canner. See the Pressure Canning recipes at the end of this book for more information on home canning beans.

Bean and Lentil Soups

GOLDEN LENTIL SOUP

This bright golden dal soup is a flavorful burst of sunshine on a cloudy day. Made with yellow lentils (dal), the warming flavors of garlic and ginger, inflammation-busting and mood-enhancing turmeric, and other delicious ingredients, you'll love serving this sunshine in a bowl.

1 tablespoon coconut oil

1 onion chopped

2 cloves garlic crushed

1 inch ginger root peeled and diced

1 teaspoon turmeric

1/4 teaspoon red pepper flakes

3 carrots, shredded

1-1/2 cup yellow lentils *also called Dal*

3 cups Chicken Broth

2 cups filtered water

13.5-ounce can full fat coconut milk

1 tablespoon sea salt, *adjust to taste*

1/2 cup unsweetened coconut flakes

1/4 cup fresh cilantro, stems removed and leaves coarsely chopped

1. In the bottom of a large stock pot or in your Instant Pot on the Saute function, melt coconut oil over medium heat.
2. Add chopped onion, garlic, and ginger root and saute until onion starts to brown, about 15 minutes.
3. Add turmeric, red pepper flakes, and shredded carrots and saute until carrots are soft, about 5 minutes.
4. Once the carrots are soft, add lentils, broth, and water, cover pot, and simmer over medium heat until lentils are soft, about 30 minutes.

Instant Pot directions: Cover, set vent to 'seal', and cook on manual (high pressure) for 10 minutes. Allow pressure to release naturally.

5. As the lentils cook, toast coconut flakes in a dry skillet over medium high heat, shaking every 30 seconds, until edges start to turn golden brown, about 5 minutes.
6. Remove coconut from heat once toasted and set aside.
7. After lentils are cooked and coconut flakes are toasted, add the canned coconut milk to the lentils and use an immersion blender to puree to desired consistency.
8. I like to leave about half the lentils whole, and only puree so half is smooth.
9. To serve, ladle lentil mixture in bowls, top with extra coconut milk if desired, and sprinkle with chopped cilantro and toasted coconut flakes.

RECIPE NOTES

If your lentils do not become soft after 30 minutes, add 1/2 teaspoon of baking soda, cover, and cook for additional 10 minutes. If they still do not become soft, consider using bottled water or a pressure to cook legumes in the future.

SPECIAL DIET NOTES:
Sprouting lentils makes them more digestable for the GAPS Diet.

GAPS

To sprout lentils: Fill a glass mason jar 1/4 to 1/3 of the way full of clean, dry lentils. Cover with filtered water and allow to soak overnight. After soaking, rinse throughly, and allow to drain. I use a mesh sprouting lid that fits onto a wide mouth mason jar to sprout. Repeat rinsing a couple times every day until small tails form, about 1/8 inch. The lentils are now sprouted and ready to use!

DAIRY FREE

BACON AND BLACK BEAN SOUP

Bacon and black bean soup is a delicious classic that is easy on the budget and high on yumminess! Soaking beans is an extra step, but it improves the digestibility of the beans (and reduces gassiness!) and lets you use those incredibly inexpensive dry beans!

MAKES 8 SERVINGS

2 cups dried black beans

16 ounces bacon chopped

1 cup chopped onion

4 cloves garlic crushed

8-10 cups beef broth

5 bay leaves

1 teaspoon honey

1 teaspoon dry mustard

1 tablespoon lime zest

1 tablespoon lime juice

1 teaspoon tobasco or other hot sauce, more to taste

Sour cream sliced green onions as additional toppings

SOAK BEANS

1. Rinse beans and place into a large bowl.
2. Cover with filtered water.
3. Allow to soak 8-12 hours, overnight.

MAKE SOUP

1. In the bottom of a low stockpot over medium heat, cook bacon.
2. As bacon is cooking, chop onion.
3. Remove bacon once desired doneness, and set aside. Add onion to bacon grease in the stock pot.
4. As onion cooks, crush garlic and add to onion.
5. Once onion is soft, drain soaked beans and add to the stock pot with the onions and garlic. Add in broth, bay leaves, honey, and dry mustard.
6. Turn heat to medium-high until soup boils, then cover and turn to a low simmer. Cook for 1 hour covered.
7. Before serving, remove from heat, add zest lime and lime juice. Serve, topping with sour cream and chopped cooked bacon as garnish.

If using the Instant Pot, follow steps 1-4 using 'saute' mode, medium heat.
Then follow steps 5 and 6, cooking under high pressure for 20 minutes, allowing pressure to release naturally before following step 7.

Nutrition (1/8 recipe) Calories 532 Fat 29g Carbohydrates 37g
Fiber 8g Protein 2g
Net Carbs: 29 g

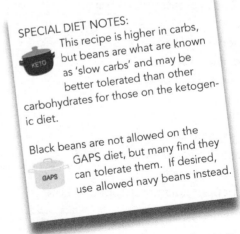
SPECIAL DIET NOTES:
This recipe is higher in carbs, but beans are what are known as 'slow carbs' and may be better tolerated than other carbohydrates for those on the ketogenic diet.

Black beans are not allowed on the GAPS diet, but many find they can tolerate them. If desired, use allowed navy beans instead.

GARBANZO LEMON SOUP

This dairy-free soup still tastes rich and creamy, thanks to the tahini and garbanzo beans. Full of fresh flavors from the lemon and dill, this is a great warming soup when you're wanting something fresh, but it's still the cold early days of spring.

SERVES 6

1 pound garbanzo beans (chickpeas), dry

1 tablespoon bacon grease or olive oil

1 onion, diced

3 carrots, peeled and diced

4 cloves garlic, minced

4-6 cups chicken or beef broth

1/3 cup tahini

1/4 – 1/2 cup lemon juice

1 tablespoon sea salt, more to taste

2 cups fresh baby spinach, loosely packed

chopped fresh dill, to taste

fresh cracked pepper or lemon-pepper, to taste

PREP STEP:

Soak your beans ahead of time to improve digestion and shorten cooking time of the soup itself.

INSTRUCTIONS

1. Soak beans overnight in filtered water.
2. Heat bacon grease or olive oil over medium heat, add onion and carrot, saute for about 5 – 7 minutes, add the garlic and saute for 1 minute more.
3. Add the broth bring to a boil, add the garbanzo beans., reduce heat to medium-low and cook, covered, for 1 hour, until garbanzo beans are soft.
4. Remove from heat, add tahini and lemon juice and salt.
5. Use an immersion blender to puree to desired thickness.
6. Add the baby spinach, give a good stir, greens will soften and wilt within a few minutes. Add as much dill as you like, and season well with salt & pepper. Soup will thicken upon standing, add more liquids as needed.
7. Serve in individual bowl topped with fresh dill.

Nutrition:
Calories 410 Fat 14g Carbohydrates 55g Fiber 15g Protein 19g

Net Carbs= 30 g

NOTE:

The herbs can be changed up to suit your taste. If you don't care for dill, try using rosemary or oregano.

DAIRY FREE

These soups can either be served on the side of the main dish, or as a starter before the main dish. Using soup as a starter is my preferred way to serve them, as I know my kiddos have had a good amount of nourishing broth and veggies before the main course.

Soup is a delicious side to many dishes including:

- Roast
- Steak
- Sandiwches
- Brazillian Cheese Bread
- Grilled or baked chicken
- And so much more!

Side dish soups are a fantastic way to use the vegetables that are seasonal for you. By using seasonal veggies you will have a natural flow where your meals change as the weather does.

Tip: The produce that is inexpensive is usually in season!

Peppers, carrots, and beets are abundant in the summer. Cool-season vegetables like kale, spinach, broccoli, and cauliflower are perfect for the 'shoulder seasons' of early spring and late fall. Then hard squash like pumpkin and butternut as well as onions store well and are so warming as we approach late fall and winter.

In addition, by using in season veggies these soups are incredably inexpensive, and because soup is so forgiving, you can use up what you have in your fridge already.

WARMING BUTTERNUT SQUASH SOUP

MAKES: 4 SERVINGS

The first winter we changed our diet to be grain-free I made this soup over and over and over, we love it! It's so warm and comforting, and with the addition of coconut milk it is rich and full of healthy fats as well.

1/2 large butternut squash or a whole medium squash peeled and cubed (1.5-2 lbs total)
3 tablespoons butter, tallow, or coconut oil
1 pint chicken broth
1 teaspoon sea salt
1 inch ginger root
2 cloves garlic
1 quart water (or to taste)
1 can coconut milk or 12 ounces heavy cream

1. Peel and cube butternut squash.
2. In a medium sized pot, melt butter over medium heat, and add the butternut squash, stirring occasionally for 10 minutes.
3. Crush the garlic and thinly dice the ginger, add, and stir for 10 more minutes.
4. Add in chicken broth, keeping the heat at medium.
5. Add salt.
6. Add water, 1 quart will make a thick soup as pictured, or add more for a more thin soup.
7. Cover and cook on medium-low for an hour, until the squash is soft.
8. Puree soup using an immersion blender.
9. Top with coconut milk or cultured cream

Nutrition per 1/4 recipe: Calories 163 Fat 10g
Carbohydrates 15g Fiber 1g Protein 4g

> **Tip:** If you hate peeling winter squash, you can bake it, cut side down in an inch of water instead, 350 degrees until soft. Then scoop the soft pulp out and use that- you're going to puree it anyway!

DAIRY FREE

NOURISHING BEET SOUP

MAKES: 4 SERVINGS

This beet soup is bright and rich, and a different flavor profile from many common winter meals. Beet soup is a delicious starter or side year round, warm or cold!

4 medium beets peeled and chopped
4 carrots peeled and chopped
3 cups broth or more to thin the soup as desired
½ teaspoon sea salt or to taste
¼ teaspoon pepper
¼ teaspoon cayenne pepper (optional)
¼ cup fresh dill finely chopped (optional)
2 cloves garlic add more to taste
Cultured cream to serve (optional)

1. Place the beets, carrots, broth, and salt in a stock pot or an Instant pot or slow cooker.
2. Cook the soup base:
   Stock pot: Bring to a boil, then reduce to a simmer (medium low heat) and cook covered for 1 hour.

   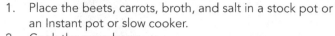 Instant Pot: Cook on high pressure for 25 minutes.

   Slow Cooker: Cook on low 8 hours or high 4 hours, until the beets are soft.
3. Add pepper, cayenne pepper, dill, and garlic and puree with an immersion blender, in a food processor, or blender. Add more broth to thin as desired.
4. Serve warm or cool and serve chilled.
5. Serve topped with yogurt or cultured cream, and additional fresh dill if desired.

Nutrition per serving:
Calories 86 Fat 1g Carbohydrates 16g Fiber 4g Protein 2g
Net carbs = 12 g

BEETS!

Beets are a love 'em or hate 'em food- I am so glad that my family all loves them though! This soup is so delicious, and beets have great detoxifying properties to support immune function, which is so needed in the winter time. This is my favorite soup for the summer too, since it's so good cold.

FRENCH-ONION SOUP

Sometimes when I'm in the mood to cook, but I don't know what to make yet, I go into the kitchen and start chopping onions as I heat a nice big pan with butter in it.

Caramelized onions are a perfect start to many recipes, from French onion soup like this one to topping hamburgers to starting the perfect roast. Nobody can ever have too many caramelized onions. In this recipe, as the onions were caramelizing for French onion soup, I prepared half a batch of Fathead Dough to be used as the topping.

Low carb, adaptable for the GAPS or SCD diets, primal, grain free, and gluten free... mozzarella dough is the perfect topping for this rich and flavorful french onion soup.

Makes 4 Servings

For the Soup:

1/2 cup butter or ghee if dairy-free
4 onions sliced
2 garlic cloves chopped or crushed
2 bay leaves
2 fresh thyme sprigs plus 2 extra for garnish, if desired
1 teaspoon sea salt + more to taste
1/2 teaspoon freshly ground black pepper
1 tablespoon apple cider vinegar or 1/4 cup red wine
2 quarts beef broth
4 ounces Gruyere cheese Or cheddar can be used

For the Fathead Dough Topping:
(this makes enough topping for 8 servings)

1-3/4 cups low-moisture (not fresh) mozzarella cheese
3/4 cup almond flour or pork rind crumbs
2 tablespoons cream cheese
1 egg

INSTRUCTIONS FOR THE SOUP

1. In a large sauce pan, or a small stock pot, or the instant pot melt butter over medium heat as you chop the onions.
2. Once butter is melted, add chopped onions (I add them as I chop them) and garlic, bay leaves, 2 thyme sprigs, salt, and pepper. Use a wooden spoon and stir every few minutes until the onions start to turn golden, about 25 minutes.
3. As your onions caramelize, prepare your fathead dough for the top. This is optional, and to make the recipe dairy-free just omit this step. The soup is still delicious, flavorful and warming without the top layer.
4. Once onions are caramelized, deglaze the pan by adding in the apple cider vinegar or red wine. Once you add the apple cider vinegar in, use a wooden spoon to scrape off all the browned bits - these are delicious concentrated flavor. This step takes about 1 minute.
5. Once the pan is deglazed, add in beef stock and simmer on low for at least 10 minutes, or until ready to serve (cover if you will be simmering it for much longer than 30 minutes).
6. To serve, taste to adjust salt and pepper if needed. Remove bay leaf and thyme sprigs. Ladle into bowls and top with broiled fathead dough, as described in the fathead step. Top with a sprig of thyme if desired as garnish and enjoy!

TO MAKE THE FATHEAD DOUGH TOPPING

1. Follow these instructions to make fathead dough. Half a recipe is a perfect amount for 4 servings of soup - to halve your egg (as called for in the recipe) just whisk an egg in a small custard cup, and only add half to the egg step. Or make a full recipe and make extra fathead shapes to use as sandwich bread or whatever you desire :) They do freeze well.
2. Form your fathead dough (also called mozzarella dough) into squares or desired shapes that are approximately the same size as the bowl you will use to serve the soup.
3. Pre-bake fathead shapes at 400* for 10 minutes and then reserve until you are ready to serve your soup.
4. Before serving, preheat broiler to high and move the oven rack to the the top of the oven. Flip over fathead dough, still keeping it on the parchment, and top evenly with grated Gruyere cheese.
5. Broil for 2 minutes, or until cheese bubbles and starts to brown. Immediately and carefully remove from oven and transfer to the top of your soup-filled bowls.

Nutrition:
Calories 558 Fat 44g Carbohydrates 13g Fiber 3g Protein 22g

10 g net carbs per serving as recipe is written. Nutrition data assumes fathead topping and cheese are used.

SPECIAL DIET NOTES:

Lower carb version: Use 2 onions instead of 4; each onion has 8 g net carbs, so by reducing the recipe to 2 onions rather than 4, you cut your net carbs to 6 net carbs.

CREAMY PEPPER SOUP

PREP TIME: 15 MINUTES COOK TIME: 1 HOUR TOTAL TIME: 1 HOUR 15 MINUTES SERVINGS: 6 SERVINGS

The roasted peppers and sweet butternut squash make an amazing rich and flavorful soup. Enjoy hot or cold the next day as well.

4 red or orange bell peppers cut in half, seeds and stems removed
1 small butternut squash 1-2 pounds, peeled and cut into 1-inch cubes
2 cloves garlic
1 quart chicken broth
1 quart filtered water
1 teaspoon sea salt
1 lemon juiced
Cultured cream to garnish

INSTRUCTIONS

1. Preheat oven to 400*. In an oven-proof stock pot, place squash cubes and de-seeded peppers. Roast for 30 minutes, the edges will start to brown on the vegetables.
2. Using oven mitts, remove stock pot and add garlic, broth, water, and sea salt. Simmer over medium heat for 30 more minutes, or until squash is soft.
3. Use an immersion blender to puree the soup right in the stock pot.
4. Add the juice of the lemon right before serving and garnish each bowl with cultured cream or heavy cream.

Nutrition:
Calories 144 Fat 2g Carbohydrates 26g Fiber 4g Protein 6g
Net carbs = 22 g

SERVING SUGGESTION

This soup is rich and full of protein and vegetables. Serve with jam-topped coconut flour bread to complement the flavors and make a fast weeknight meal.

EGG-DROP SOUP

This simple egg-drop soup is a great start to a big meal. Made with chicken broth and eggs, it gives a 'noodle' feel without the carbs. This soup is simpe and dairy-free without any adjustments.

3 cups chicken broth
2 eggs
1/8 teaspoon tumeric powdered, dried, optional for color
1 pinch pepper black or white
3 green onions

1. In a medium saucepan, heat broth over medium heat to a simmer.
2. As the broth comes to a simmer, whisk eggs, pepper, and turmeric with a fork in a small bowl or cup.
3. Once the broth is simmering, lower the heat to medium-low. Use a fork or a whisk to briskly whisk the broth in a circular pattern with one hand. With the other hand, slowly pour in the egg mixture, creating a thin stream (like pouring milk into coffee) that you whisk as it goes into the broth.
4. Once all the egg mixture is whisked in, stop whisking and allow to continue to cook until egg is cooked through, about another minute.
5. Top with optional sliced green onions and serve.

Nutrition:
Calories 90 Fat 5g Carbohydrates 3g Fiber 1g Protein 8g

DAIRY FREE

BROCCOLI-CHEDDAR SOUP

This broccoli-cheddar soup is so comforting and yummy, just the right proportion of broccoli to cheese to broth. The nutmeg included is just a tiny amount, but it gives a delightful subtle earthy flavor that really makes this soup memorable!

MAKES 4 SERVINGS

1 tablespoon melted butter
1 medium onion chopped
3 cups chicken stock recipe
1 small head fresh broccoli stem removed and florets
chopped into bite-sized pieces (about 3 cups chopped)
1 large carrot shredded
1 /4 teaspoon nutmeg
8 ounces grated sharp cheddar cheese (2 cups)
1 cup heavy cream
1/2 teaspoon sea salt or to taste

1/4 teaspoon freshly ground black pepper

1. In the bottom of a stock pot, melt butter over medium heat and add onion once chopped.
2. Saute onions until edges start to brown and onions are soft.
3. Add cream, chicken stock, chopped broccoli, and carrot, keeping on medium heat.
4. Once the soup is simmering, lower heat to medium-low and cook an additional 20 minutes, or until broccoli is soft.
5. Add nutmeg, salt, and pepper and use an immersion blender (or process a few batches through a regular blender and pour them back in) to puree the soup to desired consistency.
6. The more you puree it, the thicker it will be. I like to leave some chunks for texture, but have it mostly smooth and creamy.
7. Stir in grated cheddar cheese, reserving a little to top the bowls of soup with as garnish. Serve immediately.

*Take care not to heat the soup to a boil after adding the cheese or the cheese will break down and the texture will be clumpy and grainy.

Nutrition:
Calories 482 Fat 44g Carbohydrates 5g Fiber 1g Protein 17g

Net carbs= 4 g

Instant Pot Directions: Use the saute function rather than a stock pot on the stovetop. Do not pressure cook the soup; it will over cook the broccoli.

LOADED CAULIFLOWER SOUP

This soup tastes and looks just like a loaded baked potato, but with a veggie-rich low carb base of pureed cauliflower with the perfect savory seasonings. Top however you like, and turn into a meal by adding a little crumbled sausage to the base of cauliflower after pureeing.

MAKES 8 SERVINGS

1/2 pound bacon

1 onion

4 cloves garlic

2 lbs frozen cauliflower or one head of fresh cauliflower

1 quart chicken or beef broth

1 teaspoon sea salt, to taste

1/2 teaspoon black pepper, to taste

1 teaspoon dried chives

8 ounces cream cheese

4 ounces sharp cheddar cheese

4 green onions, just the light green and white parts

Jalapeno slices, optional

Sour cream, optional

1. Chop bacon into 1-inch pieces.
2. Heat a stock pot over medium heat and cook bacon until cooked through to your desired doneness. As the bacon cooks, peel and chop the onion and peel and crush the garlic.
3. Remove bacon and set aside, leaving bacon grease in the stock pot.
4. To the bacon grease, still over medium heat, add 1 chopped onion and 4 cloves crushed garlic. Stir occasionally for 20 minutes, until fragrant and onion starts to brown.
5. Add cauliflower, broth, sea salt, black pepper, and chives., Cook over medium-high, covered, until cauliflower is soft; approx 20 minutes. As this is cooking, shred the cheddar cheese and slice green onions and optional jalapenos.
6. Lower the heat to medium-low and add in the cream cheese and shredded cheese. Stir gently and continue cooking until heated through and the cheese melts in.
7. Serve, topping with green onions, jalapenos, sour cream, and the bacon you set aside. Enjoy!

Nutrition: Calories 323, Fat 26g, Carbohydrates 11g, Fiber 3g, Protein 12g

Net Carbs= 8 g

DAIRY-FREE MUSHROOM SOUP

Rich in subtle earthy flavor from 4 kinds of mushrooms, this cream of mushroom soup recipe is simple to make and absolutely swoon worthy. It is a lovely healthy alternative to canned cream of mushroom soup. We make it gluten-free, keto, paleo, and GAPS friendly by thickening just with the mushrooms themselves, which puree into a delicious thick creamy and flavorful soup.

Coconut milk is used to make the soup creamy, add nourishing fats, and keep this soup dairy free. The sage and black pepper keep the coconut flavor from overpowering.

DAIRY
FREE

MAKES 6 SERVINGS

2 tablespoons ghee or avocado oil
1 yellow onion diced
2-3 cups fresh mushrooms or 1 to 1-1/2 cups dried (a combination of portabella, white button, shiitake, oyster, or other mushrooms that are available to you)
4 cups chicken broth
2 cups filtered water
1 tablespoon fresh sage very thinly sliced, or 1/2 teaspoon dried/ground sage
1 bay leaf
1 teaspoon sea salt or to taste
1/4 teaspoon freshly ground black pepper or to taste
1 cup full fat coconut milk plus a bit more to garnish if desired.

1. In a stock pot, heat ghee or avocado oil over medium heat. Peel and chop onion. Saute chopped onion in ghee or oil as you slice mushrooms.

2. Slice mushrooms and add to the onions after about 10 minutes. Continue cooking both onions and mushrooms until soft, another 10 minutes.

3. Add chicken broth, water, sage, bay leaf, sea salt, and pepper, keeping on medium heat.

4. Once the soup is simmering, lower heat to medium-low and cook an additional 20 minutes. Puree with an immersion blender, or in batches in a regular blender.

5. Remove bay leaf and serve, garnishing with sliced sage and extra coconut milk if desired.

Nutrition: Calories 190, Fat 15g, Carbohydrates 9g, Fiber 2g, Protein 5g

Net carbs: 7g

RECIPE NOTES

1. If you eat dairy, you can use heavy cream in place of the coconut milk. Both are delicious!

2. To use this mushroom soup recipe in place of cream-of-mushroom soup in a recipe, omit water and puree well.

MUSHROOMS
Commonly found in grocery stores

Button Mushrooms: Button mushrooms, also called white mushrooms, are the most common mushrooms used in the US. They are delicious and take on the flavors of any dish they are in.

Crimini: Also called Italian Brown or Baby Portabello, Crimini mushrooms are more rich in flavor than button mushrooms, but still easily adaptable to all dishes.

Portabello: These mushrooms are fully mature Crimini mushrooms, and hold up well to cooking and stuffing. They are large- hamburger bun size- and make a great low-carb gluten-free bun alternative!

Shittake: Native to Japan, shittake mushrooms are more earthy in flavor and add a delicious savory flavor to dishes.

Oyster: These mushrooms can be found growing in the wild, and are readily availble cultivated in many grocery stores. They give a slight anise flavor and creamy texture when cooked.

Dried Mixes: Dried mushrooms may be easier to find than fresh, and an easy way to keep delicious unique mushrooms on hand.

QUICK PUMPKIN SOUP

This delicious soup can be made all from scratch, or you can whip it up quickly using pre-made broth, a can of pumpkin, and a can of coconut milk!

MAKES: 4 Servings

15 ounces cooked pumpkin
13.5 ounces coconut milk full fat, reserve some for garnish if desired
2 cups chicken broth
2 cups water
1 teaspoon sea salt
2 cloves garlic

1. Crush garlic, and combine all ingredients in a medium saucepan.
2. Heat soup over medium-low heat for 10-20 minutes, stirring with a wooden spoon every few minutes. Cover with a lid to speed the heating, remove lid to stir.
3. Serve and enjoy!

Notes:
Garnish with a drizzle of reserved coconut milk and flat parsley leaves or sprinkle of roasted hulled pumpkin seeds if desired.

Nutrition: Calories 301, Fat 24g Carbohydrates 12g Fiber 5g Protein 6g

Net carbs= 7

CLASSIC FLAKEY BISCUITS

These are perfect flakey biscuits to eat with soup.

Biscuits are best made by getting your hands all into the butter and flour to combine. If you don't like touching your food as you make it, a pastry blender can be used - but trust me, the best results come from using your fingers to find clumps of butter and work it into the flour.

This recipe might be a surprise to you here- we do eat wheat flour occasionally as a treat, and these biscuits are one of our favorites!

INGREDIENTS
2 cups all purpose flour
2-1/2 teaspoons baking powder
1/2 teaspoon sea salt
5 tablespoons butter cold, cut into pieces
2 tablespoons sugar or honey, optional
3/4 cup half and half

1. Preheat oven to 425° F. Line a baking sheet with parchment paper.
2. In a large mixing bowl, combine flour, baking powder, and sea salt.
3. Cut cold butter into pieces- about 16 pieces per stick (cut lengthwise and then at each tablespoon marker). Butter must be cold or your biscuits will not have the correct texture.
4. Drop a few pieces of butter into your flour mixture at a time, and toss gently - like you're coating chicken for frying. You don't want the butter to clump together, but instead want to have it evenly distributed in the flour.
5. Next, use your fingers to work the flour into the butter, until about half the mixture resembles breadcrumbs, but the other half still contains pea-sized pieces of butter. This takes about 5 minutes. Do not use a stand mixer for this step or your biscuits will be tough. A pastry blender can be used instead of your fingers if desired.
6. Once the butter and flour is combined, sprinkle with optional sugar or honey. Add in all the half and half and mix with a fork, gently, and without overmixing.
7. Add up to 3 tablespoons additional half and half as needed to make a stiff dough that just holds together for rolled biscuits, or a slightly more wet dough (cookie dough consistency) for drop biscuits, see below.
8. For flakey rolled biscuits (my favorite!), divide dough into 2 halves, and roll to 1-1/2 inches thick between two pieces of parchment paper. If dough is tacky, sprinkle 1-2 tablespoons flour over the top, but do not add too much flour.
9. After rolling out, cut into desired shapes - we usually just cut into equal rectangles or squares, but cookie cutters can be used for extra special biscuits.
10. Brush off excess flour after rolling out. Tops can be sprinkled with sugar or cinnamon-sugar if desired.
11. Transfer biscuits to prepared cookie sheet, leaving 1-1/2-2 inches between biscuits. Bake on the center rack for 12-18 minutes, until the corners turn golden brown and the biscuit is cooked through. Cool for 5 minutes on the cookie sheet and serve.

For drop biscuits: (faster, but less flakey), mix in additional 1/4-1/2 cup half and half. Use a soup spoon or serving spoon to drop 1/4-cup portions of biscuit dough on the prepared cookie sheet 2 inches apart and bake as directed for rolled biscuits in step 11 above.

Nutrition Per Biscuit
Calories 145 Fat 7g Carbohydrates 19g Fiber 1g Protein 3g

Canning is an art and a hobby:

Think of canning as a productive hobby more than a kitchen shortcut, this will give you the perserverance to continue through the canner troubleshooting that often comes with your first few batches of canning.

These steps may feel overwhelming as you read through them. Once you have done the process a few times it will become much more natural. Watching your pantry fill, and enjoying tender delicious meals that are so fast to heat and serve is incredibly rewarding.

Once you work out all the kinks with your canners, and have a few favorite recipes up your sleeve, it becomes second nature to can up some extra meat, broth, beans, or vegetables as you prepare dinner during a free afternoon or evening.

PRESSURE CANNING SOUP

LET'S GET STARTED

Seeing pre-made shelf-stable soup lined up in my cabinet makes my heart flutter with joy. If you too get excited at the idea of your shelves lined up with homemade soup read ahead, I think you will be surprised at how straightforward pressure canning actually is!

Temperatures above boiling, glass jars, and whizzing steam, gauges, releases, and technicalities- isn't pressure canning best left to those who are kitchen pros? Not at all!

Pressure canning now is much easier than you may be picturing. Modern pressure cookers have multiple safety features and are much easier to use than you probably are expecting.

You CAN pressure can:

1. Broth
2. Meat
3. Vegetables (though not all will taste good canned)
4. Fruits (though we won't be covering that here)
5. Beans
6. Seasonings and spices with any of the above

You can NOT pressure can:

1. Cream or dairy
2. Coconut milk
3. Grains or pasta
4. Pureed soups or vegetables (pre-mashed potatoes, pureed squash, etc- special processing is needed to reach the middle of thick purees.

You will not LIKE pressure canned:

5. Broccoli, cauliflower, or brussels sprouts; they lose their shape and taste really sulfur-y when canned.
6. Leafy greens like spinach, chard, or kale, they do not hold their shape in the high heat and turn bitter.
7. Most herbs and spices, they become bitter and are best added during heating or while serving.
8. Some people like them, but many do not like canned peas, they turn mushy and lose their flavor.

Good for us, our pantry, and our grocery bill, many of the soups we eat, or their base parts, are completely pressure-cannable and delicious canned!

Dairy (cream, cheese, cream cheese, sour cream) can be added to soup after re-heating.

Canned broth makes for easy soup without having to reduce broth down or store in the freezer. Vegetables can also be canned using broth as their liquid, making them a simple homemade soup in a jar. Take advantage of the summer garden, seasonal produce, and farmers markets by canning excess food in season for use through the year.

I love canning especially because I can control the ingredients and I know exactly what is in my canned soup, how much salt is used, and how high quality the meat was that made the broth.

STOVETOPS

Most home stovestops are just fine for pressure canning, but we will cover potential issues with different stovetops below.

GAS STOVESTOPS: The ease of adjusting the heat with gas stovetops makes them the easiest to use with a pressure canner so that you can keep consistent temperature, and lower it easily when you need to. *Watch for:* The amount of space between your stovetop and vent hood or cabinet- if this is short, you may need a smaller canner.

ELECTROIC STOVESTOPS: Electric stovetops with the common coil heat source are also great for canning. No adjustments are needed. *Watch for:* The amount of space between your stovetop and vent hood or cabinet- if this is short, you may need a smaller canner.

GLASS STOVETOPS: Glass stovetops can be used for canning, but check with your stove's manual. Also, even if okay for canning, be careful to not move/slide a hot full canner across the top, as this has shattered glass stovetops on rare occasions.

INDUCTION STOVETOPS: There are adaptors that can make an induction stovetop work for canning, but getting a seperate burner is usually recommended instead, due to the slight chance of shattering the stovetop if the hot canner is moved.

SPECIAL EQUIPMENT
for Pressure Canning

Pressure Canner: Pressure canning has to come to a specific pressure, and though the principals are similar, pressure canning *cannot* be done in an Instant Pot other than the Instant Pot Max at the time of this writing.

Cost saving tip: I borrowed my first pressure canner to try it out and see whether it was something I enjoyed doing, and my family enjoyed eating the results. I was instantly hooked, and soon went out to buy my own. Borrowing before buying is always recommended!

Canning jars: Quart, Pint, wide mouth, regular mouth. You are only limited in size by what fits in your canner. Jars can be stacked in most canners too, so if single serving canning works better for you, go on ahead and stock up with pint jars!

Canning rings: Don't stock up on canning rings and lids, you actually want to take the rings off after canning and store your filled sealed jars with just the lids, then you can reuse the rings over and over.

Canning jar lids: Go with well known canning jar lid (the flat part) brands Ball or Kerr, some of the new and lesser known brands don't have as reliable of a seal. You'll need new lids each time, this ends up being our only ongoing expense for canning other than a small amount of electricity or gas needed for the stovetop. I find that Walmart often has lids when other places often only sell the ring/lid sets.

BASIC STEPS for *Pressure Canning*

Wash Jars: Because we bring pressure-canned jars up to such a high temperature, we only need to wash them rather than steralize. A dishwasher is just fine for cleaning!

Prepare Food: Undercooked, cooked, or sometimes raw food is canned. Prepare your food as indicated on the recipe you are using. It should be noted that there are lots of conflicting opinions when it comes to canning food. For this book we are using the USDA guidelines, which have been extensively tested and studied and found to be safe over and over.

All food to be canned should be of good quality, and produce should be scrubbed clean, or peeled.

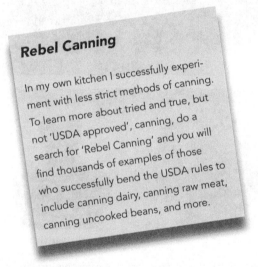

Rebel Canning

In my own kitchen I successfully experiment with less strict methods of canning. To learn more about tried and true, but not 'USDA approved', canning, do a search for 'Rebel Canning' and you will find thousands of examples of those who successfully bend the USDA rules to include canning dairy, canning raw meat, canning uncooked beans, and more.

Add Water to Canner:
Add recommended amount of water to the canner; usualy this is 2 inches from the bottom of the canner, without the jars in it. Unlike water bath canning, we do NOT need the water to cover the top of the jars when using a pressure canner.

Tip: If you have hard water and your jars come out of the canner with a white film, adding a teaspoon of cream of tartar to the water in the bottom of the canner will prevent this hard water buildup and give you sparkling clean jars to store.

Pre-Heat Jars and Canner If Needed: Hot jars go into a hot canner, cold jars go into a cold canner. If you are pre-heating your canner, make sure you also are pre-heating your jars and your food is hot. You can keep your jars in a closed dishwasher to keep them warm, or add them right side up to your canner as it pre-heats.

Pre-heat your canner by filling with recomended amount of water, and then heating it on medium heat with the vent open.

This pre-heating prevents the shock (and cracking of jars) as a cold jar goes into a hot canner, or hot jar goes into a cold canner.

Fill Jars: Use a funnel or canning funnel (where the opening is wide and fits just inside your canning jars) for ease of transfer to your jars. Fill your jars with hot cooked or raw food, as indicated in the recipe you are following.

Clean Jar Rim: Use a damp paper towel or damp clean towel to wipe the rims of the jar before adding the lids. This makes sure a good seal is formed.

Screw on lids and Rings Use new, washed, lids and new or used rings. Tighten well, but do not use excess force to tighten the rings onto the jars.

Place Filled Jars in the Canner: Add recommended amount of water to canner (usually 2 inches) if you haven't already done this. Place your jars evenly into your canner, with the rack on the bottom if specified by your canner instructions.

Vent Canner for 10 minutes: Place lid on your canner, but keep the vent cap off. Bring up to a boil gently, usually over medium heat, and allow to vent for 10 minutes, or what is specified in your canner's instructions.

This allows the canner to fill with steam and eliminates air pockets within the canner, which can preven the canner from coming up to the correct temperature.

Place Vent Cap on and Bring to Pressure: Place your vent cap on, it may look like the one to the right, or may be another shape or dial (below). If it is weighted, place it on your vent cap so that the desired weight is down.

Allow canner to come up to the correct pressure for your altitude.

Troubleshooting: If your canner does not reach the correct pressure within 20 minutes, your heat may be tooo low. You want to gently bring the temperature up and down, so usually you will avoid putting the heat on 'high' but raise the temperature to medium-high and see if that helps.

If the canner still will not come up to pressure, the lid and gaskets may need to be greased. Follow the directions in your canner's directions to do this.

Can Food for Time Indicated in Recipe: Keeping at a consistent pressure as necessary for your altitude, cook food for the time indicated in the recipe.

As you get a feel for canning you will know what your canner sounds like when it is at the correct pressure, and what setting on your stovetop will maintain the correct pressure. Until you are more experienced with your canner, make sure to check on your canner and see that it is maintaining pressure every few minutes during the canning process, adjusting the heat up and down slightly to raise or lower the pressure as needed.

Turn Off Heat: Once the time has been reached for your canning, turn off the heat under your canner but keep the lid on and vent cover on. It is now safe to walk away from your canner. Allow the pressure to come down on its own, this often takes an hour or more. Once pressure is at '0' you can remove the vent cap. Allow stem to escape for another 10 minutes, or longer, and then remove the lid, being careful to tilt the lid away from you as hot steam will be coming out.

Allow the jars to stay in the canner undistrubed for another half an hour or so. The jars can be left in the open canner overnight if needed.

Remove Jars from Canner: After allowing the jars to sit in the canner with the lid open, you can then move the jars to a dish towel that is placed on the counter. Leave the jars on the towel on the counter for a full 24 hours.

You may hear the 'pings' as the lids seal during this time. They may sound like they are sealing and unsealing during this time, this is okay as long as the indent in the lid is down the next day, indicating that they did indeed seal.

Store Your Canned Food: After allowing the newly canned food to sit undisturbed for 24 hours, a good seal should have been made! Check for the seal by pressing the center of each lid. There should be no movement when pressed down, indicating a good seal.

Clean jars if needed using a rag and warm water with some dish soap, under running water.

If some of the liquid siphoned out (ended up in the canner) the jars are still okay as long as they sealed. Usually siphoning, or cracking, is the result of raising or lowering the temperature too fast. Next time use a lower temperature when bringing your canner up to pressure.

If any jars did not seal, transfer to the refridgerator and eat within 1 week.

For the jars that did seal, remove the rings, label the lid with the contents and date, and store in a cool dark place for up to one year.

As you add jars of canned food to your pantry, bring the older food to the front for use first and place the new food in the back.

PRESSURE CANNED BROTH

If you only learn how to pressure can one recipe, let it be broth! Canned broth makes nourishing soup in seconds, and when you can broth it stays at room temp- so no more storing and thawing heavy frozen jars or bags.

INGREDIENTS

2 quarts broth or more, adjust the amount of jars you use to accomidate.

    See recipe for Beef Broth (p. 15) or Chicken Broth (p. 16) or Fish broth (p. 51)

2 teaspoons sea salt optional

INSTRUCTIONS

1. Pre-heat jars and lids to hot but not boiling.
2. Pre-heat pressure canner over medium heat with 3-4 quarts water, or the amount indicated by your pressure canner's manual.
3. Add hot broth to each jar, leaving 1 inch at the top. This is called headspace.
4. Add 1/2 teaspoon sea salt (optional) to each pint jar.
5. Use a clean towel dipped in vinegar to wipe the rim of each filled jar. Top with lids and screw on bands until firmly secured but not over tightened. As tight as you can get them without really forcing anything is just fine.
6. Place hot jars in hot canner and secure lid on canner. Turn heat to high.
7. Once steam is coming out of the vent pipe, allow to vent with steam coming out for 10 minutes.
8. Cover the vent pipe with the counter weight (dial gauges) or weighted gague (jiggler)
9. Once proper pressure is reached, process for indicated time below.
10. After the time has been reached at the proper pressure, remove from heat by either lifting off the electric burner or turning off the gas.
11. Allow canner to de-pressurize on its own, do not open the vent pipe. This takes about 30-45 minutes.
12. Once depressurized, remove jars carefully and allow to cool 1 inch apart on a cooling rack or folded towel. Once cool check lids for seal. If they are sealed, your broth is now good for 1 year at room temperature! Remove rings before storing.

PRESSURE & TIME

Pressure: Under 1,000 feet 10 lbs Over 1,000 feet 15 lbs

Time: Pint jars 20 minutes, quart jars 25 minutes. *If mixing pint and quart jars in the same canner, process all for the longer time

 Tag me on Instagram with pictures, I'd love to see your canning progress! @healthhomeandhappiness or #healthhomeandhappiness

PRESSURE-CANNED KIDNEY BEANS

There are so many reasons to home-can beans. The cost savings is significant, and you get to control the liquid used (we use nourishing broth here), the kind of salt used, and the container is glass- no questionable BPA can lining. This process is fast, and when you have home-canned beans, legume-based soups come together super quick! They're also a perfect side dish or addition to taco night!

Any kind of dried beans can be used in this recipe with no adjustments. We are using Kidney Beans here, as called for in our Every Week Red Chili, page 20.

INGREDIENTS

1 pound dried kidney beans
1 quart broth, chicken or beef
Filtered water as needed to cover beans
(1/2 teaspoon sea salt per pint jar) (optional)

INSTRUCTIONS

COOK THE BEANS:

1. Place dried beans or peas in a large pot and cover with water.
2. Soak 12 to 18 hours in a cool place. Drain water.
3. Cover soaked beans with broth and filtered water and boil 30 minutes.

CAN THE BEANS:

1. Pre-heat jars and lids to hot but not boiling.
2. Pre-heat pressure canner over medium heat with 3-4 quarts water, or the amount indicated by your pressure canner's manual.
3. Fill jars with beans and cooking liquid, leaving 1-inch headspace.
4. Add ½ teaspoon of salt per pint or 1 teaspoon per quart to the jar, if desired.
5. Use a clean towel dipped in vinegar to wipe the rim of each filled jar. Top with lids and screw on bands until firmly secured but not over tightened. As tight as you can get them without really forcing anything is just fine.
6. Place hot jars in hot canner and secure lid on canner. Turn heat to high.
7. Once steam is coming out of the vent pipe, allow to vent with steam coming out for 10 minutes.
8. Cover the vent pipe with the counter weight (dial gauge) or weighted gague (jiggler)
9. Once proper pressure is reached, process for indicated time below.
10. After the time has been reached at the proper pressure, remove from heat by either lifting off the electric burner or turning off the gas.
11. Allow canner to de-pressurize on its own, do not open the vent pipe. This takes about 30-45 minutes.
12. Once depressurized, remove jars carefully and allow to cool 1 inch apart on a cooling rack or folded towel. Once cool check lids for seal. If they are sealed, your beans are now good for 1 year at room temperature! Remove rings before storing.

PRESSURE & TIME

Pressure: Under 1,000 feet 10 lbs Over 1,000 feet 15 lbs

Time: Pint jars 75 minutes, quart jars 90 minutes. *If mixing pint and quart jars, process all for the longer time

PRESSURE CANNED BASIC GROUND BEEF AND VEGETA-BLE SOUP

SERVINGS: 4 SERVINGS

This pressure canned basic beef and vegetables soup is delicious, filling, inexpensive, and made with easy-to-find ingredients. The extra portion of ground beef makes it extra filling!

INGREDIENTS

2 tablespoons butter or avocado oil

1 yellow onion peeled and chopped

2 pounds ground beef

2 teaspoons sea salt

1/2 teaspoon ground black pepper

1/2 teaspoon dried thyme (optional)

1/4 teaspoon dried oregano (optional)

2 carrots

4 stalks celery

4 cups beef broth

14 ounces canned diced tomatoes not drained or one pound fresh tomatoes, chopped and seeds removed

INSTRUCTIONS

1. In a large pan or stock pot, melt buter and cook onion and add ground beef and seasonings. Slightly brown ground beef.
2. Preheat jars and canner.
3. Place beef, onions, and seaonings the bottom of hot jars, filling about 1/3 of the way loosely packed.
4. Add raw vegetables to be 2/3 full.
5. Cover with hot broth, leaving 1 inch of head space.
6. Pressure cook as detailed on pages 78-79.

PRESSURE & TIME:

Pressure: Under 1,000 feet 10 lbs Over 1,000 feet 15 lbs

Can pints for 75 minutes, quarts at 90 minutes.

PRESSURE CANNED CARROTS IN BROTH

Pressure canned carrots make for a fast side dish, or quick additions to soup or roasts. My kids love to help can carrots by using the crinkle cutter, available inexpensively on Amazon or at kitchen supply stores. See soupchallenge.net for a link to buy.

This is a raw-pack recipe, so a great one to start with since you don't need to mess with hot jars or pre-heating your canner.

You can use water to can with, but here we use broth for the nutrition boost.

Makes: 4 quarts or 8 pints canned carrots, or increase or decrease quantities as desired

Ingredients:
10 lbs carrots
2 quarts pre-made broth
4 teaspoons sea salt (optional, and only if using unsalted broth)

1. Heat broth over medium heat until hot. As broth heats, wash and cut your carrots.
2. Scrub and peel carrots. Slice or dice as desired.
3. Raw pack – Fill jars tightly with raw carrots, leaving 1-inch headspace.
4. Add 1 teaspoon of salt per quart to the jar, if desired.
5. Add hot broth or water, leaving 1-inch headspace.
6. Wipe jar rim with a clean towel dipped in vinegar.
7. Add lids and rings lids and process as detailed on pages 78-79, using the pressure and time below.

PRESSURE & TIME:

Pressure: Under 1,000 feet 10 lbs Over 1,000 feet 15 lbs

Time: Pint jars 25 minutes, quart jars 30 minutes. *If mixing pint and quart jars, process all for the longer time

SERVING SUGGESTION:

For a fast pureed soup, add garlic or your seasoning of choice, and you have a delicious carrot soup shelf stable in the pantry ready to go!

PRESSURE CANNED
SIMPLE HEARTY BEEF STEW

Prep Time: 30 Minutes MAKES: 3 QUARTS

Pressure-canned stew is a classic, and a great quick meal for any time! We love to bring it camping for homemade taste in a complete ready to eat shelf stable jar. The stew meat is usually inexpensive, and really the tough cuts excel in this recipe as the pressure cooking transforms them beautifully into tender delicious bites.

2 pounds stew meat cut into 1-inch cubes

1 tablespoon tallow or other cooking fat

1/2 teaspoon freshly ground black pepper

1-1/2 teaspoons sea salt

2 large onions chopped into one-inch pieces

3 large carrots scrubbed and chopped into one-inch pieces

6 stalks celery scrubbed and chopped into one-inch pieces

1 six-ounce can tomato paste

2 cups homemade chicken or beef broth, unsalted

INSTRUCTIONS

1. Heat a pan or Instant Pot to medium high and melt fat in the bottom.
2. Once the fat is melted, add beef and sprinkle beef with salt and pepper.
3. Brown beef on all sides, stirring every 5 minutes or so with a wooden spoon. Beef should be brown in about 15 minutes. Chop your vegetables while you brown the meat.
4. Add onion, carrots, and celery and stir to mix into the meat.
5. In a large saucepan mix tomato paste and broth and heat over medium-high heat.
6. Place beef, onions, and seaonings the bottom of jars, filling about 1/3 of the way loosely packed. Add raw vegetables to be 2/3 full. Cover with hot broth, leaving 1 inch of head space.
7. Wipe jar rim with a clean towel dipped in vinegar.
8. Add lids and rings lids and process as detailed on pages 78-79, using the pressure and time below.

PRESSURE & TIME:

Pressure: Under 1,000 feet 10 lbs Over 1,000 feet 15 lbs

Can pints for 75 minutes, quarts at 90 minutes.

Freezer DIY 'Instant' Soup Packs

These soup packs make it a snap to make soup for either main dishes, or a side dish or starter. This is a fantastic way to get broth in your diet for easy-to-absorb amino acids, and tons of vegetables for vitamins, minerals, and fiber. Plus the soup packs are gorgeous and rewarding to make . Follow these directions to make 6 different soups that would feed a family of 4.

If you want to cook less at a time, simply make the same amount, but use quart zip-top bags rather than gallon bags.

Ingredients/Grocery List

For the broth cubes:
1 pot chicken or beef broth (page 14-16)
1 cup Grassfed Beef Gelatin

A combination of vegetables that are in season, inexpensive, and your family's preference.
Used in this example:
4 butternut squash
6-10 onions
1 bunch celery
6 Anaheim chilies
5-10 lbs carrots

Also good, but not specifically called for in the following directions: (5 lbs is a good amount): Broccoli, cauliflower, summer squash, green beans, celery root, beets.

Seasonings:
1/4 cup sea salt
Smoked Paprika
Cayenne Pepper
Basil
Oregano
Granulated Garlic
Ginger

Directions for Soup Packs:

1. Reduce broth to 2-3 quarts by simmering on low over the stove top or in the instant pot, with lid off.
2. Allow broth to cool.
3. Once cooled to room temp, add gelatin and mix in with a whisk or fork. Allow gelatin to absorb liquid.
4. Preheat oven to 425* If you have a convection oven, use the convection setting.
5. Peel and chop onions.
6. Rinse, deseed, and chop peppers.
7. Place chopped onions and peppers on a baking sheet, sprinkle with about 1 tablespoon sea salt.
8. Roast onions and peppers in the oven.
9. Once gelatin has absorbed the broth and is thick, heat over medium-low heat for 15 minutes, or until melted.
10. Continue rinsing, peeling, and chopping other vegetables.
11. Once gelatin is melted, remove from heat and allow to cool. Transfer to fridge once close to room temperature (or cover and place outside where the cold winter air can cool it for free!)
12. Roast the rest of the vegetables in shallow pans or dishes in the same manner as the onions and peppers.
13. Roast with similar colors together.
14. Once vegetables are starting to brown at the edges (about 20 minutes of roasting), remove from oven and put new vegetables in until all vegetables have been roasted.
15. Allow vegetables to cool.
16. Once gelatin/broth mixture is solidified, cut into 2"x2" squares. These are your broth cubes that will be included with your vegetables in the freezer bags.
17. Transfer vegetables to bags in desired amounts and combinations and ½-1 teaspoon of 2-3 of the seasonings, in different combinations as desired (suggestions on next page)
18. Add one-two broth cubes to each bag, evenly distributing among vegetables.
19. Add 1 teaspoon fine sea salt or 2 teaspoons coarse sea salt to each gallon bag, or half as much if you are using quart-sized bags.

Soup instructions (all soups):

1. Fill a saucepan, stock pot, or slow cooker ½ to ¾ full with vegetables and broth cube from the soup pack.
2. Cover frozen vegetables with filtered water.
3. Slow cooker: Cook on low for 8-10 hours, high for 4-6.
4. Stove top: Cook over medium heat, covered, until brought to a simmer.
5. Reduce heat to low and cook an additional 30 minutes, until heated through.

Flavor combinations and serving instructions:

*** Add 1 teaspoon fine sea salt or 2 teaspoons coarse sea salt to each gallon bag as you add the broth cube. Add more salt after cooking, to taste.

Curried Butternut Squash:

1 part onion
4 parts butternut squash
1 teaspoon ginger
1 tablespoon granulated garlic
Top with coconut milk after pureeing.

Classic Chicken Soup:

1 part each of the vegetables
1 tablespoon dried basil
1 teaspoon dried oregano
1 pound boneless/skinless chicken, or 2 cups leftover cooked chicken.
After cooking, do not puree.
Add 2 cups cooked, diced chicken during the last 20 minutes of cooking. Squeeze the juice of 1/2 fresh lemon over each bowl.

French Onion Soup

3 parts onions
Optional: 1 part green beans
Garnish with shredded parmesan, if you eat dairy, to serve.

Carrot-Butternut Soup

2 parts roasted carrots
2 parts roasted butternut squash
1 part onions
1 teaspoon smoked paprika
Cook, then puree with an immersion blender.
Top with a sprinkle of paprika and dollop of yogurt before serving.

Cream of Celery

2 parts celery
1 part onions
1/2 teaspoon dried coriander OR thyme

Puree this soup after cooking. Garnish with sour cream or coconut milk.

Ginger Beef

1 part onions
2 parts carrots (if you did broccoli and/or cauliflower, use in place of the carrots)
1 inch fresh ginger, grated, or 1/2 teaspoon powdered ginger

To serve:
1/2 teaspoon freshly ground black pepper
Pinch sea salt
1 pound grassfed beef steak
1 tablespoon tallow, butter, ghee, or coconut oil
Half an hour before dinner, season the beef with salt and pepper and cook over medium high heat for 5 minutes in a skillet in melted fat.
Flip over once browned, reduce heat to medium-low, and then continue cooking until cooked through (10-15 minutes- it will depend on the thickness of your steak)

Index

Cheesesteak 37

Made in the USA
Las Vegas, NV
09 September 2023

77333454R00050